EXPERT AN
OWNER'S (

Founder-ow
New York City, Pat Widmer handles thousands
of cats each year and answers cat owners'
questions every day. In direct, easy-to-
understand language, she gives specific,
straightforward information about—

—What to feed a cat, and how much

—How to spot health problems, and what to
   do about them

—Why a cat should be neutered or spayed

—What the truth is about declawing

—How to train your cat: punishment vs.
   correction

—How to deal with special situations: a new
   baby, a handicapped cat, moving to a new
   home, taming a wild cat, the cat's place in
   your love life . . . and much more expert
   advice you never found in a cat book
   before!

PAT WIDMER'S CAT BOOK

PATRICIA P. WIDMER is the founder-owner of Pet Clinicare, a
low-cost spray-neuter clinic in New York City's Manhattan.
She is a guest lecturer at the University of Pennsylvania
School of Veterinary Medicine, appears often with pets on
television talk shows, and for seven years directed the New
York City pet-owner education program. She also writes a
question-and-answer column each month for the *Humane
News* and is the author of *Pat Widmer's Dog Training Book*,
also available in a Signet edition.

Pat Widmer's Cat Book

STRAIGHT TALK FOR CITY AND SUBURBAN CAT OWNERS

by
Patricia P. Widmer

Foreword by Lee Bernstein,
Executive Director,
Associated Humane Societies

Photographs by Ilene Jones

A SIGNET BOOK

NEW AMERICAN LIBRARY

CONTENTS

v

CONTENTS

Contents

FOREWORD

It has finally been written: a complete book on cats, from soup to nuts. In her usual face-the-facts way, Pat Widmer has done it again (her first book was *Pat Widmer's Dog Training Book*).

Widmer tells it as it is in straight, concise, easy reading, sprinkled with Widmer humor, that sets the record right once and for all on such important issues as spaying, declawing, grooming, feeding, de-allergizing, behavior, and much, much more. Nothing is missed! The book is written in clear, easy-to-understand language. Your interest never falters throughout.

The best thing about this book is that if you had questions about cats before, they will be answered now. If you had doubts about adopting a cat, you'll run out and get one. But don't do it until you have read every page. Increased cat adoptions are sure to result, as will better living for those cats already in homes; and I can't tell you how happy this makes me!

—Lee Bernstein
Executive Director
Associated Humane Societies

Jasmine sunbathes in Pet Clinicare's front window. She was abandoned at the clinic, leukemia positive, now negative.

INTRODUCTION

Over thirty years ago, when I graduated from sixth grade, my classmates gave me a book on dogs with an inscription indicating their belief that I should become a veterinarian. I knew that was one thing I should never do because my low tolerance for suffering then, as now, would not permit.

But with the passage of years and despite a very high-pressure business career, I was always animal-involved, eventually leaving the business community totally to pursue animal activities of many types. Dog training served to convince me that dogs should be neutered for their own peace of mind as well as for health and overpopulation considerations. So I began demanding neutering as a prerequisite to training assignments.

Shortly thereafter, I became heavily involved as a volunteer in two humane organizations: the ASPCA, and a private death camp for animals outside the city. The great amount of time I spent at these two institutions convinced me that the most pressing need in the animal world today is cheap, readily available neutering. It was clear to me that neither killing nor stockpiling was a solution. And the sight of hundreds of bodies stacked in the morgue at the ASPCA really propelled me to action.

By 1977–1978, veterinarians nationwide had already declared their animosity toward low-cost spay/neuter.* The humane organizations for the most part were paying lip service, no more. But the City of Los Angeles had three clinics, obviously successful. A Vancouver, British Columbia, humane organization opened one with even greater success. On Long Island the Scully Clinic functioned beautifully. And in New York City, even with so-called "professional consideration," I was paying $150 for a dog spay with inoculations; $100 for a cat castration, declaw, inoculations. Like every other animal worker, I was limited to what I could afford, not what needed to be done. Although local humane organization leaders talked spay/neuter, no clinic was in the offing, and the stray population was growing. The ASPCA/city-government solution was to pay roundup agents on a per-head incentive basis to pick up animals to be killed.

By April 1978 I had incorporated Pet Clinicare as a not-for-profit organization in New York State, leased an old film building on the West Side of Manhattan and with the help of friends started total renovation of the building, hiring of veterinarians, and ordering of equipment and supplies. The clinic opened June 1, 1978, offering dog and cat spay and neuter and cat declaw at rates averaging one-quarter to one-third those elsewhere in the city.

Within a month we learned there would be fifteen to twenty cats for every dog, and we ordered cat cages by the dozen. Although I had spent years

*"According to the Executive Board decision, AVMA will actively oppose all current spay and neuter clinic bills, except the Koch bill, HR2828, which AVMA will neither actively oppose nor support." *Journal of the American Veterinary Medical Association*, vol. 171, no. 7 (October 1977), p. 597. The Koch bill included every measure the AVMA had demanded.

working with dogs and cats and was owned by both, nothing provided the education built into running a clinic handling hundreds of animals a week, answering questions from the public, hiring and working with veterinarians, and caring for the animals themselves seven days a week.

Many of the cats abandoned at the clinic had health problems, notably feline leukemia, and we became very much involved in diet and vitamin therapy since the veterinary community had nothing to offer in the way of a cure through "hard drugs."

Until September 1979 the most exciting event in my life was the opening of the clinic itself and the giant step forward it represented. However, in September 1979 we learned quite by chance that the megavitamin treatment we were using with our leukemia cats had successfully changed several positives to negative. It was a joy beyond description. Since then we have seen many other cats recover from a variety of illnesses as a result of the same therapy. But it always remains a delight to be able to bring about major change in the animal community through low-cost neutering and to be able to help each animal directly through behavioral and health-care advice.

All of the many things learned every day at Pet Clinicare have been incorporated into this book in the ways that our thousands of clients find most usable. The sequence of presentation is important. If you skip sections or jump to the section you think you need, you will not have a complete picture; whatever smidgen of advice you follow will probably not work. So please do read the chapters in order.

Cats seem very complex, often obscure creatures because we have not given them or our relationship with them sufficient observation. It has also been convenient and often profitable for the cat to remain a mystery and for all sorts of superstitions and myths to be perpetuated. For this reason I have included not only the truths about cats but also a great deal of debunking. A little—or should I say *a lot*—of light on the subject means a much greater number of healthy, happy, *living* cats, off the streets, purring contentedly on your sofa and mine. If this is not sufficient cause for us to learn and reason together, what is?

1

CAPTURED BY A CAT?

Captured by a cat? Or ten ... or twenty ... or thirty ... or more? One of the wonders of the feline is that the average cat owner has more cats than the dog owner has dogs or the parent has children. And nary an eye is batted!

Usually we simply accept these truly extraordinary companions into our lives and only with the loss of one or a notable behavioral problem do we become sufficiently introspective to consider how such tiny creatures take over our heart and too often, our will. And the more we *consider*, the less we seem to *know*; then the thoughtful moment passes, and the mystery remains.

Until the next time ... which in the multiple-cat household in the multiple-cat community arises before you know it. And the questions pique us again occasioned by a newly arrived stray, a cat dying as the result of leukemia, a living room "sprayed" into oblivion, a litter of kittens with no prospective homes.

What *is* the nature of the cat, what makes the cat so special, so different from man's other pets?

If 'tis true that the domestic animal—our pet—is a divine gift to show humans their own reflection, how could we *possibly* seem to see such different reflections from our dogs and cats? Could it be that

Thomas, once a filthy, battered, leukemia-positive parking-lot tough, now presides over Pet Clinicare's front desk, instructing clients in the proper care of their pets and dispensing flea collars. His appearance is impeccable except that he has not learned to keep his bow tie straight.

dogs reflect our "personalities" (outer selves) and cats our "character" (inner being)?

We certainly develop different relationships with each. Dogs accompany us everywhere—everywhere our personality is manifest—and become involved in our relationship with the world in general. But cats remain in our homes, where our character dominates and our secret self lives. Too, we tend deliberately to train our dogs, go to them, and impose our standards upon them. It's only natural since we have to housebreak them and housebreaking necessitates teaching the dog to walk on a leash, urinate and defecate outside on our schedule and terms. Dogs commonly being a good deal larger than cats, we also expect far more in terms of general behavior (no, my eighty-five-pound dog may *not* walk across the dining table).

Since the vast majority of cats litter-train themselves, to some degree or other, we may never have to come to grips with housebreaking, certainly not with leash-training. We really never quite develop or even think of the same human-dominated relationships with our cats. Then *we* sit around and say *cats* are independent, untrainable, and so forth.

They may well be sitting there saying humans are independent, untraining (after all, if you trained your dog or helped your child with his homework in front of your cat, what else could the cat say?), and so forth.

As we explore the feline-human relationship, keep in mind how little effort you probably have made at communication, rule setting, understanding—leaving the cat to his own devices and expecting everything to turn out the way you want it. Even though you weren't completely sure *how* you wanted it.

Now you have picked up this book either out of general interest in cats, as the result of questions about your cats, or even in desperation because the cats are running your life in totally unacceptable terms and you know you must get things under control. Next you'll begin expecting things of your cats, and they will sit around and say, "Are you kidding? We've been doing things our way for the last four years. You're going to have to work awfully hard to earn our respect and cooperation."

You actually must decide how you want things and then go all out to convince the cats you're serious. Some cats take a lot of convincing!

The Feline Essence

Like all animals, including humans, cats have instincts which cannot be contravened. Instinctive behavior can be channeled in any way that coincides with the instinct. You cannot, however, expect to go against instinct and win with anything less than brute force. So all efforts set forth in this book are directed at making the cat's instincts work for you and for your cat as well. I will never suggest you go against instinct; that would be useless, cruel, and an enormous waste of time and effort.

Within nature there is a very rigid social structure. Each species has its place, and within the species each animal has its niche. We all realize that each species is dominated by some species and itself dominates others. And if we think about it, we realize that each animal *within a species* dominates some and is dominated by others. Man included. It is only natural that one species be dominated by a bigger or smarter species. We humans are both bigger and smarter (?) than the cat, and most of our other pets for that matter. This is appropriate. It is the human role to be responsible for the other animals

Marshmallow

in the creation, and to be responsible, we must dominate, *like it or not!*

Dominance

But how to do so . . .

In just the ways you would with another human or pet. Eye contact is primary. When you want to dominate anyone, you look him in the eye. His looking away indicates there will be no challenge. Interestingly enough, even when there is no vision, there is still the attempt (and success) to dominate via eye contact. My tough, blind street cat "stares" at other animals and knows they will back away, run off in terror.

So start looking your cats in the eye, addressing
each by name (no matter how many you have!), and
putting yourself in the leadership role. Frequently,
a good stern look will deter an action the cat already knows to be unacceptable, just as a loving
glance lets a cat know he is welcome in your lap or
on the bed.

Voice is also a most common means of dominance as well as communication. You have undoubtedly noticed that your cats have learned a lot of
basic words and commands—the ones that happen
to suit them. Now you start adding the ones that
suit you.

Another form of dominance is physical: hand on
scruff of neck or via the collar—and when necessary,
the leash. A mother cat lifts her young, moves them
around, corrects them, and punishes them by picking them up by the scruff of the neck, shaking them
when she is displeased, tossing them around when
she is truly angry. It is not likely that all of you will
dominate your cats by picking them up by the scruff
of the neck, but anyone can use a collar efficiently.
One way or another, you will arrive at the means to
dominate your cats effectively and get life under
control, vis-à-vis the cats at least.

The Dependency Relationship
and the Responsibility
That Goes with It

Along with the human role of dominance as regards
domestic pets goes the pet's role of dependency
upon us for food, shelter, protection. If you're react-

ing with "But cats are independent by nature," you will have to reconsider. Cats (and all other living creatures) need food, shelter, and protection from natural and man-made enemies.

Living in a human environment, they certainly cannot be expected to supply their own food. If they could, there would not be millions of cats starving to death in this country. In your role of supplier-of-food, however, remember that in nature, food is never provided for any animal without effort on its part; nor is food constantly available. The animal must make an effort to hunt in order to secure food. Your cat may not have to scavenge for food, but he should at least know that he is fed at your pleasure, that he is fed once a day if adult, that he is fed the amount appropriate to his size and age, that he will not find food sitting around to be eaten at whim, that he will not be overfed so that he has no dependency upon his owner.

It is *very* important that your cat not only be dependent but that he *know* he is dependent upon you for food. The principal reason fat cats are so nasty, lazy, and independent is that they don't need their owners. A week after he goes on a rigid diet, your average obese cat becomes friendly and much less independent. Two months later he is interesting, interacts with humans and other animals constantly, is handleable, *is* and *knows* he is dependent. Appropriate perspective has been restored!

Shelter is a factor that permits few alternatives. You take a cat in and keep him in. The shelter is permanent, and he will take it for granted, as do you except when you're making a mortgage payment.

Protection, however, is a whole other thing. The principal reason you keep the cat inside is to pro-

"The Gang" with tails raised in anticipation of breakfast.

tect him from disease, cars, other animals. You provide regular inoculations and other veterinary care in order to protect him. As pack leader, you permit no aggression among animals in your home so that all may live in peace under your beneficence.

It is an absolute necessity that all pets be aware of your dominance, protection, and role as provider. This is your position as the human, and abdicating in favor of the animals is extremely upsetting to them inasmuch as it is completely contrary to nature.

If you're like most, you are at this point thinking how easy a particular cat was at a certain age, how things changed, how other cats seem not to have changed in the same way, and so forth. Such recollections are confusing until you get a little perspective on cat behavior and begin to see the patterns that have developed around you.

Because we live in a society very much taken with the "superiority" of the human species and ofttimes forgetful of the important roles animals play (no, we could not do without them in any sense), even the most cat-involved frequently do not give cats enough credit for intelligence, character, personality. Oh yes, we have many cute stories and occasionally some downright awe. But few really notice how personality actually develops and changes with age, environment, structure, diet, and so on. Rather, what they don't like becomes part of the "nasty cat," and what they do like is the "nice cat." Of course, the "nasty cat" was named Hitler at six weeks of age, when he *wasn't* nasty. And the "nice cat" has always been called Samantha.

Nasty cats can become nice cats. And nice cats can all too readily become nasty cats through lack of objectivity, lack of understanding, or lack of appropriate action on the owner's part.

Coming of Age

So, to begin at the beginning.

Kittens under six weeks of age are interested in their moms and brothers and sisters—mainly Mom, because she supplies food, warmth, direction. Brothers and sisters are just part of the scene for the first few weeks and then become playmates around four weeks of age. By six weeks kittens are physically and mentally able to leave home—leave Mom, that is—and start eating and living on their own. At this point they are kitten-oriented if they have other kittens around; dog-oriented, if there are dogs. Without other kittens or pups, they become somewhat people-oriented. I say "somewhat" because they become people-oriented for lack of an alternative. But understand, it can be *any* people—basically, whoever feeds them. In playing, kittens play with objects, not people. If the people play with toys, the kitten joins in and plays with the toys. She will play with a human hand or finger sometimes for lack of a better toy—not by choice of a human toy!

As kittens reach twelve weeks of age, they begin to take interest in humans. Much as you would like to think the kitten attaches herself to you, she doesn't really. She just begins to have interest in another species—human, whatever. She is less self-centered.

It is important right here for you to come to grips with another point: all animals except man live in the present moment. They do not relive the past or dream about the future. Lucky creatures! This is why they don't need gurus to teach them to meditate, to achieve "oneness," "nowness." They have it all already.

So if you are in the moment with your kitten, you're it. Any human being, however, may replace another at this stage so long as the kitten's needs for food, warmth, litter, attention are met. As the cat matures, say from five or six months of age on, she becomes more discriminating. She will attach herself to people who meet her psychological needs as well as bodily requirements. She develops her own personality at this stage and is not just another cute, playful kitten. She has character now and is a more interesting being, seeking another such in human relationships. This is truly the age at which anyone who knows cats well would begin to consider taking a particular cat into a household if it were totally a matter of choice. In other words, before this age, you don't know what you get and will have to deal later with the personality and make the cat live within the boundaries you set. But when a cat is beyond five months of age, you pretty much know to begin with what she will be like and whether she is what you seek in the way of personality—soft, affectionate, demanding, independent, clinging.

Then somewhere between five months and a year we hit another stage: adolescence, teenage if you will. Your cat still has the personality you know, but she doesn't have much time for you because she has other things to do *all the time*—usually playing.

You will suddenly feel you have lost your cat. She may even quit sleeping on the bed or show up only for meals—even though she's only in the next room. As the months pass, you will probably acquire another cat *for yourself*. That's okay. By the time the new one reaches the same stage (she will), all of a sudden the previous tomboy is back in your lap, back on your pillow. You won't believe your eyes. But it's real. They a.. come back. The moral? DON'T GET RID OF A CAT DURING THE TEEN-AGE PERIOD. It's perfectly natural, and the cat will come around eventually—sometimes in six months, sometimes a year.

Unfortunately, all these changes happen at the time when males become male and females go into season. Make sure the cat is neutered by now. Otherwise you'll have an unhappy, perhaps even nasty, independent, unaffectionate cat. Be aware, also, that this is the stage when the cat is no longer growing and doesn't need the quantities of food previously required. Cut back substantially on diet—to one meal a day, approximately one-third cup of dry food, total—or you will have an overweight (FAT) cat. Fat cats are slow, ugly, dull, NASTY, and short-lived. They also have housebreaking problems, severe health problems (urinary-trace blockage in males being the most instantly life-threatening), shed more, and so forth and so on. Nobody needs a fat teenager!

The best advice I could give anyone would be to adopt a cat over five or six months of age, have her neutered if she is not already, feed her moderately, live through the teenage period whenever it strikes, and enjoy fifteen to twenty years with the perfect cat.

As an aside I might confirm that most of my cats came to me when anywhere from a year to ten years of age. Kittens get adopted out because everyone thinks they want them (I know better) and because young cats can go live anywhere instantly and form new attachments. Adult cats will attach themselves to the first good human being who comes along and are very discriminating thereafter about accepting new owners. That's why it's so easy to adopt a homeless or ill-treated cat. Do a few things right, and you have loyalty for life in the form of a faultless feline.

The Social Graces

In addition to the stages of life that interest and perplex us, there are quite a few social graces we particularly love in our cats that distinguish them from our other animal friends. But we are frequently unsure of the meaning of these gestures.

Licking

Although your cat's sandpaper tongue may not please you too much, you must consider licking as just a sign of affection and then extricate yourself the best way possible when it all reaches the unbearable point. Cats naturally groom one another by licking, but when this gesture is extended to humans, it is probably more likely to be submissive. That is appropriate since the human should be the dominant one. But the roughness of the tongue imposes its own limits!

Purring

Think cats purr when they're happy? Right. But they also purr when excited, hungry, angry, fearful. Actually, "purring" is a noise made by the cat while breathing. As you get to know your cat, you will hear different types of purrs, different levels of vibration. The purr of a cat is a great sound to go to sleep by!

Raising Hindquarters and Tail

As a normal sign of affection or desire to be petted or fed, cats raise their hindquarters and tail. Oddly enough, having done so, large numbers of them will then bite you if you stroke the rear half of the back. It's quite normal, does not indicate your spayed female is in season, that your male is a female, or anything else except anticipation of food or attention.

Kneading

Most cats "knead"—that is, push against things with alternating front feet—anything and everything just as if they were making bread. Some knead favorite pillows, favorite people, other cats or dogs. A few never knead. All must have done so, or tried to, at an early stage in life since kittens knead their mother's breasts when nursing, supposedly to make the milk flow. However, I have several cats that definitely nursed for months, but rarely knead, and several at the other end of the spectrum. I have also seen kittens nurse without kneading. Kneading people is generally thought of as a sign of affection and acceptance. At this point all I know is Marshmallow cat will knead my left shoulder indefinitely if I let her, but unfortunately, I occasionally need some sleep. She is always disappointed, sometimes graciously, sometimes not.

Not surprisingly, all of these normal activities are acceptable to us, even when overdone and annoying! So we move along and consider at greater length the behavior that is not acceptable and evidences something amiss between cat and human.

First, though, we will deal with the many physical-mechanical facets of caring for a cat so that errors in those areas will not further compound the behavioral problems most often created by human misunderstanding of the most perfect of creatures, the cat.

2

CARE

URI FVR-CP FeLV FIP
Feline Health

Looks like a crazy cryptogram or a bad set of Scrabble letters, doesn't it? Actually, these are all health concerns to the cat owner. But to start at the beginning:

FVR-CP

Kittens need to be vaccinated on a schedule beginning at six weeks of age. When you acquire a kitten, consult a veterinarian immediately and let him or her advise you. Adult cats need a vaccination each year; two inoculations, spaced two to four weeks apart, are given the first time around. The vaccination, called FVR-CP, is for rhinotracheitis, calici, panleukopenia viruses. Pneumonitis vaccine is available and is given if there is reason for concern with that disease, but it is not routinely given because of the short duration of effectiveness (four to five months) of current vaccines. Rabies vaccine is given cats who may come in contact with rabies virus. It is most important that the vaccine, FVR-CP, be given yearly, more often if you take in new cats from time

Marshmallow kneading, kneading, kneading . . .

to time. The viruses in question are airborne, and
even closely house-confined cats may contract them

Worms and Other Parasites

When you take your cat in for a vaccination
make sure he gets a thorough checkup, including
examination of a fecal sample for worms and othe

parasites. (You must take the stool sample in with
you. Get it from the litter the previous night, wrap it
well, and store it in the refrigerator overnight in
case there is none in the morning. If you need to
check one particular pet's stool for worms or other
medical problems, feed that pet alone, having put
two or three drops of green food coloring in his
food. His stool later that day and the following one
will be green.) This may reveal roundworm, hook-
worm, or coccidia, all harmful parasites effectively
treated with medication. Tapeworm is not usually
revealed in a microscopic examination of the stool.
It is diagnosed by seeing small white particles around
the rectum or on the stool. These particles look like
grains of rice and are actually segments of the worm.
If you see them, advise your veterinarian and secure
tapeworm medication. Tapeworms are usually contracted by the cat's eating a flea that is host to
tapeworm. So treat a flea infestation at the same
time. If the infestation has been severe, you may
have to treat the cat for tapeworm several times. So
treat the flea infestation to begin with. Your veterinarian can help you in this regard. Be aware,
however, that many commercial flea preparations
are lethal to cats and must be used with caution and
veterinary advice. Don't buy casually in a pet shop!

URI

Cats appear to get colds. Actually, the symptoms
indicate upper respiratory infection which must be
treated. If your cat sneezes or has runny eyes, is
eating normally, has no other symptoms, and has
been vaccinated within the past year, you can probably treat quite successfully with 500 mg. of vitamin

C (this may be purchased in any drugstore or health-food store in the same form we use, either liquid, crystals, or pills) four to five times a day until several days after the symptoms disappear. (See the section "Medicating a Cat" on page 36 for details.) If your cat sneezes or has runny eyes and has not been vaccinated within the past year, or if it vomits or has diarrhea or loses its appetite, consult your veterinarian promptly. Cats are very subtle animals, susceptible to many respiratory and gastrointestinal diseases that can be fatal if not treated promptly. The symptoms for most of these conditions are similar, so it is purposeless to try to distinguish among them in a book. Veterinary care is called for. It is usually quite easy to prevent upper respiratory infections by adding Vitamin C to your cat's daily diet. (See Diet, page 51.)

Blockages and Cystitis

Male cats and sometimes females, neutered and unneutered, are prone to urinary-tract blockage. You will notice the cat squatting repeatedly in the litter, trying to urinate but unable to do so. This situation may be followed by loss of appetite, eventually by vomiting. The cat should be treated by a veterinarian the moment you see him squatting repeatedly, unable to urinate. Urinary blockages, if untreated, are quickly fatal because the body, unable to excrete via urine, becomes toxic. If you have a cat that has had urinary blockage problems, make sure he stays very thin and active, give him 500 mg. of vitamin C twice a day (this may be purchased in any drugstore or health-food store in the same form we use, either liquid, crystals, or pills). I cannot stress enough the need to prevent further blockage. Most cats, once blocked, block again and again. They cannot tolerate repeated blockages and surgery to create a new urinary opening and often die. You must prevent further blockages by keeping him thin and providing vitamin C.

Obviously, preventing the development of a blockage condition in a cat who has no history of it is possible also by keeping the cat thin and active and providing 500 mg. of vitamin C at least once daily.

A similar situation is cystitis. The cat, male or female, will use the litter repeatedly and may also urinate around the house, often eliminating slightly bloody urine. Again, veterinary care is necessary, or you can generally treat at home with 500 mg. of citamin C every few hours. And again, keeping the cat thin, active, and on vitamin C daily is good treatment and prevention. Be aware that cats are more prone to cystitis with the onset of winter weather if they go outdoors or if the house is cold and damp, so increase the vitamin C quantities at this time.

FeLV

Mention feline leukemia and get instant response from a cat lover who recently watched an adored pet waste away and die as the result of this dread disease. What is it?

Feline leukemia is a viral disease of a contagious nature. That is, one cat may pick up the virus by coming into contact with the urine, feces, or saliva of an infected cat, or a kitten may contract the disease in utero (before birth) from its mother. The contagion rate is said to be one in three; somewhere

between 10 and 30 percent of all cats currently
carry the virus. It is contagious *only among cats*.

Whether or not a cat does carry the virus may be
ascertained by a simple blood test. There are cur
rently two widely used tests: one sold by Pitman
Moore, Inc., which may be performed in a laboratory
or in the veterinarian's office, and one performed
only on the premises of a laboratory such as the
Veterinary Reference Service in Salt Lake City; Na
tional Veterinary Laboratory in Franklin Lakes, New
Jersey; or the Cornell Diagnostic Laboratory in Ithaca.
The test manufactured by Pitman-Moore is highly
sensitive and for this reason is likely to indicate the
presence of the virus at an early stage. The other
test does not generally indicate the presence of the
virus until there is a high degree of infection.

Cats found to be carrying the virus are rated as
"positive." Cats not carrying the virus are rated as
"negative." Since the incubation period is thought
to be at least three months, a cat cannot be tested
definitively less than three months after its last possible exposure to another cat or the outside world in
general.

It is important to understand that a positive cat
will not die from leukemia. The related disease from
which it may die is lymphosarcoma. However, a
positive cat—no matter how healthy appearing—is
very vulnerable to every passing disease and should
therefore be isolated and treated *even if showing no
signs of any disease!*

Until very recently there was no "cure" or "treatment" for feline leukemia. I can happily report from
my own experience with cats that there now is, and
it is simply a megavitamin food supplement which
is cheap, easy to administer, palatable, and readily

available from its originator on the West Coast. This supplement is called Mega C Plus and is manufactured by Orthomolecular Specialties, P.O. Box 32232, San Jose, Calif. 95111 (telephone 408-227-8844).

It appears necessary to use fairly high dosages of Mega C Plus to reverse a positive to negative and then to reduce the dosages very slowly to a maintenance level. Specifically, a very symptomatic (sick) cat was given one teaspoon Mega C Plus powder in his daily food and ½cc. Mega C drops six to eight times a day for six weeks and regained his health and then tested negative for the virus. His dosage was gradually reduced to ¼cc. three or four times a day plus one teaspoon Mega C Plus powder daily and is now being reduced still further to maintenance on the powder form of Mega C Plus (which is much cheaper).

We have also had excellent results with two newer therapies used in conjunction with the Mega C:

(a) An injection of 3 cc. Lactated Ringers mixed with 3 cc. sodium ascorbate is given once daily (more often if the cat is very ill) subcutaneously between the shoulder blades of the cat. (The treatment is effective for viruses other than leukemia.) You will have to have a veterinarian or other medical practitioner teach you to do this, but it is no more difficult than treating a diabetic cat with insulin injections. Either your vet or your own doctor can secure the "ingredients" for you. I prefer the sodium ascorbate currently sold by Henry Schein, 5 Harbor Drive, Port Washington, N.Y. 11050 (516-621-4300), because it is free of harmful additives.

(b) I began experimenting with Interferon in 1982 and believe it has been helpful for the leukemia cats. It may be ordered by your veterinarian from

American Interhealth, P.O. Box 734, Melbourne, Fla. 32951 (305-725-6588). It is manufactured in tablets that are given once a day crushed in food. The 1983 cost is $11 for a bottle of thirty tablets.

Asymptomatic (healthy) positive cats can be treated by feeding one teaspoon of the powder in food daily over six weeks to six months. The reversal from positive to negative may be accomplished more quickly by use of the drops every few hours for the first few days. It is necessary in all cases to continue the maintenance level of the powder thereafter. It should also be noted that too drastic a reduction in levels of this megavitamin therapy will result in the cat's going positive again. Additionally, you must realize that just as dosages are decreased gradually, they should likewise be built up gradually over a few days or weeks in order to avoid diarrhea, as indicated on the product label.

As a side benefit the product also seems to prevent urinary-tract problems, formation of bladder stones, constipation, and respiratory diseases.

All these benefits evidently result from the product's stimulating ("potentiating") the body's own immune system—not from any direct effects upon the virus or other organism. THIS DOES NOT ELIMINATE THE NEED FOR VACCINATION OR OTHER BASIC PREVENTIVE CARE. It does, however, indicate that Mega C Plus is ineffective if used with any drugs affecting the immune system, such as antibiotics and corticosteroids.

Now that you have this encouraging information, I hope you will face the testing process with the knowledge that having positive cats is not the end of the world. Have your cats tested.

Separate out the positives from the negatives. If

you have the financial resources required, you will put the positives on the liquid Mega C as well as the powder to reverse them to negative relatively quickly. Otherwise, you will use the less-expensive powder alone—it may just take longer. At the same time you will feed your negatives the powder to prevent their going positive. Once the positives go negative, you can put all cats back together but continue the liquid form for the previous positives, decreasing it slightly as time goes by, and putting the powder form in everyone's food. Eventually, the former positives will all be on the powder only, just like the other negatives.

There may well be some *severely* symptomatic positive cats in whom the virus has become so virulent that the most you can expect in the near-term future is to stimulate their immune systems sufficiently for them to regain their health and the virus to become inactive. They may continue to test positive for a prolonged period, even years. But they are the picture of health and will lead normal, healthy lives if you maintain their Mega C Plus therapy.

Together with providing Mega C Plus, you must supply a proper diet to maximize the effects of the vitamin supplement. Science Diet Feline Dry Food (obtainable from feed dealers) not only provides high-level nutrition but also prevents the diarrhea often associated with feline leukemia and/or vitamin C therapy. In addition, the diarrhea may be controlled by adding ½ or 1 teaspoon of acidophilus powder to the food daily. It restores friendly flora to the intestines. Not only is it beneficial to health but cats love it! Feeding junk food when trying to correct a serious condition only worsens matters and must be avoided.

On occasion, with particularly delicate, troubled cats, I use a totally natural diet, which I would recommend to anyone in a position to prepare fresh food for his or her cat(s). It consists of the following:

½ cup cooked oatmeal*
2 tablespoons wheat germ*
2 tablespoons chopped raw carrots
2 tablespoons Brewers Yeast (primary grown)*
200 I.U. vitamin E*
1 tablespoon Mega C Plus powder
1 tablespoon acidophilus powder*
2 large slightly cooked chicken livers
Sufficient chicken broth to mix

Mix all ingredients well. Serve at room temperature. This quantity will be sufficient to feed two cats for one day. For a very sick cat, add 2,500-5,000 I.U. vitamin A from fish oil per day.

Whenever you acquire a new cat, isolate and test it. If it's positive, keep it separate and treat it until negative. Then integrate, as above.

We recommend that you keep all your cats on a minimum of ½ teaspoon a day of the powder if they are likely always to be subject to the addition of new cats and will therefore need this protection. Orthomolecular also makes a VCM (vitamin C maintenance) powder for cats in households not subject to new cats or other stress and disease. You may wish to write them about it if your cats live in such conditions.

No one with cats can afford to neglect the threat of feline leukemia. If you feel you cannot afford to test your cats because of sheer numbers and

*May be purchased in any health food store.

economics, at the very least provide the Mega C Plus powder for them on a daily basis. You owe it to them and yourself, as the millions can tell you who have watched entire households of cats die of this disease.*

FIP

Another contagious, fatal disease for which Mega C Plus therapy appears effective is feline infectious peritonitis. In this case, the abdomen fills up with fluid as time goes by. The cat will begin to appear generally unhealthy, may wheeze or seem to choke, as if it had asthma. It may eventually have difficulty eating. (There is also a "dry" form of the disease, but the symptoms and result are the same.) Cats suspected of having FIP should not be mixed with healthy cats. The condition is not communicable to humans or animals other than cats. Interestingly, 50 percent or more of cats having FIP are positive for the leukemia virus also.

Cardiomyopathy

Another subtle killer of cats is cardiomyopathy. It is a condition in which the muscle of the heart becomes either too flabby to pump blood or too hard and contracted to do so. Most commonly, the owner is not aware the condition exists and the cat

*If you are interested in nutritional and megavitamin prevention and treatment of cancer, you will appreciate Dr. Richard A. Passwater's book Cancer and Its Nutritional Therapies, Pivot Original Health Edition 1978, published by Keats Publishing, Inc., 36 Grove Street, New Canaan, Conn. 06840. This book, available at health-food and book stores as well as from the publisher, presents an easily understood overview.

seems to die suddenly. If there are signs of the
disease, they are inactivity, labored breathing. One
form of the disease (hypertrophic) may be treated if
the signs are noticed and the cat presented for
treatment. At most the treatment will give the cat
some months or a year of life. There is no cure at
present. It is thought that cardiomyopathy is heredi-
tary since it is particularly common in Siamese or
Burmese cats. It does not appear to be contagious.

Stress

Stress is of course not a disease, but it is a major
contributing factor in the development of disease
and prevents successful treatment. For that reason it
is certainly worthy of consideration along with the
diseases it affects.

Examples of stress are:

- Subjecting a cat to aggression from persons
or other pets
- Keeping a cat caged unnecessarily for the
owner's convenience or the veterinarian's profit
- An unspayed female cat's being in season
- An uncastrated male cat's frustration
- A cat prohibited the owner's principal living quarters and companionship because it claws,
has housebreaking problems, or is ungroomed
and sheds
- A stray's living on the streets, subject to
weather, starvation, breeding, disease
- The owner's acting as if cutting nails,
grooming, bathing, vet visits, and such were of
life-threatening proportion. We see so much of
this behavior at Pet Clinicare that if an owner
comes in in a great dither, huffing and puffing

about "poor Kitty" and "how hard it was to get
him in the carrier," we mark the cage card
"STRESS" and let the cat relax for some hours
before anesthesia and surgery.

Dehydration

All of our major religions and philosophies regard water as "the great purifier." Indeed, it is,
quite literally as well as figuratively. None of us
may live without it, nor may our pets. Yet you may
have heard all the stories we have to the effect that
cats don't drink water. But cats certainly do need
water and do drink water, the quantity dependent
upon the air temperature and the cat's diet, age, and
activity level.

Normal healthy cats drink water as needed. Dehydration sets in, however, when health fails and the
cat drinks insufficient water or its body does not
utilize the water normally. Dehydration is one of
the earliest symptoms of many feline illnesses and
one that can cause quick deterioration and death if
not attended to promptly. The cause must be diagnosed and treated; fluids must be administered to
the cat as well, either subcutaneously (under the
skin) or intravenously, as the veterinarian believes
best. You cannot correct this condition yourself at
home; immediate veterinary care is called for.

The fact that professional care is required does
not mean you yourself cannot determine that a cat
is dehydrated or judge the severity of the situation.

When you take a normal healthy cat by the back
of the neck, you get a handful of skin that has good
elasticity. On a dehydrated cat, there is very little to
get hold of, and elasticity is lacking. The skin is

tight over the frame of the body. Of course, if you have a fat cat, it is also difficult to get hold of loose skin because there isn't any—it's all filled up with fat! But there still will be elasticity to some degree as long as the fat cat is not dehydrated. Just another reason for your fat cat to lose weight!

If you have many cats and must constantly be on the lookout for health problems among them, you might ask your vet to show you how to determine dehydration so you have no doubts. Your ability to do so will serve this practitioner well also, so don't hesitate.

Gingivitis

Gingivitis is a condition in which the gums become inflamed, swollen. Often teeth have rotted, the mouth is infected, the cat in pain, unwilling and unable to eat. Frequently there is also a foul odor to the mouth. In most cases, dental work under anesthesia must be performed to clean up the mouth and the cat thereafter given oral antibiotics to clear up infection. Feeding dry food will usually prevent this condition. Supplementing with 500 mg. of Vitamin C twice daily both treats and prevents gingivitis. Since gingivitis often is also an indication of feline leukemia, any cat suffering from this condition should be tested for leukemia even if soft food is suspected as the cause.

Mites

Many cats have ear mites which cause great discomfort to the cat and if left untreated may result in the cat's doing serious damage to itself (called self-trauma). These small parasites, manifest as black, crumbly material inside the ears, bite and cause the cat to shake its head and eventually scratch at its ears. Cats with claws on their rear feet will often dig deeply into the skin around the ears, inflicting severe injuries upon themselves, even shredding their ears. Your veterinarian can provide medication that kills mites. (At Pet Clinicare we have tried every product currently available and prefer Mitox for ease, effectiveness, and low cost.) Generally, it must be put in the cat's ears every third day or so, the dead mites to be cleaned out each time with a cot-

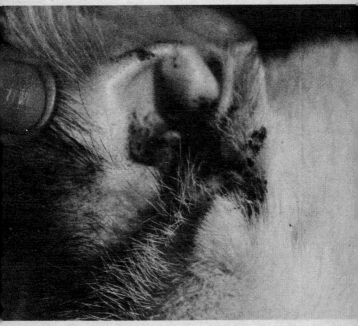

Ear mites are manifest as black, crumbly material in a cat's ears.

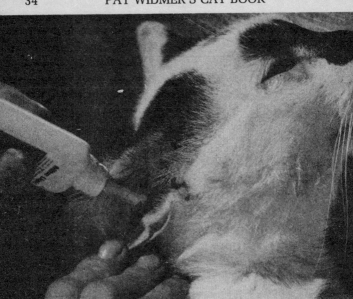

Ear mite medication is put into the cat's ear every third day.

Ear mite medication is massaged in ear.

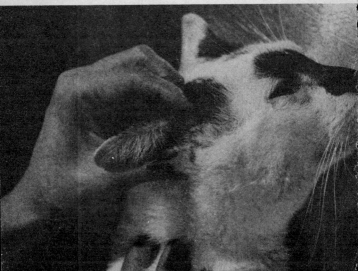

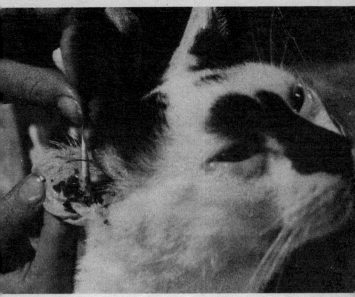

After massaging mite medication in ear, remove mites gently with cotton swabs.

ton swab. Do this for at least three weeks in order to kill eggs that may be hatching as well as the adult mites. And don't forget that mites spread from pet to pet. All dogs and cats in the house must be treated simultaneously; otherwise the parasites will simply continue to spread.

Because the ears already trouble the cat substantially, he will not be terribly receptive to treatment. If he has claws, you may wish to wrap him in a heavy towel or blanket to prevent his scratching you. In any case, proceed gently but firmly. The ears must be treated. And while you're at it, cut his nails well back in an effort to limit the damage he can do himself (see page 92).

Tiger cat removed part of his left ear scratching at mites.

Medicating a Cat

If you have reason to medicate your cat orally, you may find it not the easiest trick in the world. Some cats are pilled by pinching in the corners of the mouth between your fingers and prying the mouth open. The pill is then popped onto the very back of the tongue, mouth closed, and throat stroked to make the cat swallow. When a cat resists this method, particularly your inserting your fingers into its mouth to deposit the pill, you may find it advisable to buy a small, curved hemostat. A surgical supply house will have one, or your veterinarian may sell you one. Use it to deposit the pill on the back of the cat's tongue.

If you must give a cat liquid medication, use a *small* syringe and squirt the liquid slowly into the corner of the mouth so that the cat must swallow it.

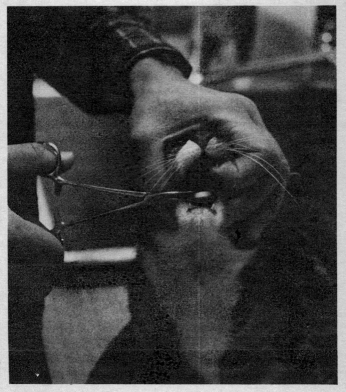

Effective way to give cat a pill is to use a curved hemostat to place the pill on the back of the cat's tongue.

In all probability you will have to medicate a cat at one time or another, so face up to it and learn how. Obviously, the process is a lot easier if the cat is declawed.

Emergency Care for Sick Cats

When a cat gets sick, it can get very sick in a hurry—much more so than a dog, for instance. Cats really are fragile.

You must take particular care that your cat eats regularly, does not become finicky from overfeeding. It is awfully hard to judge the health of a finicky, overfed cat. It also is awfully hard to get the cat eating, when ill. And eat it must when sickness threatens. A cat who does not eat rapidly becomes dehydrated and dies. You may find yourself having to force-feed a cat; the veterinarian may have to give it subcutaneous or intravenous fluids—normal procedures with a sick cat. The lack of such feeding and fluids would very quickly result in death.

You must also be prepared to take your cat's temperature as an indication of its general health. This may be done with a rectal thermometer coated with Vaseline℗. Normal is 101.5° F (38.6° C). Anything over 103° F (39° C) is cause for immediate concern and action.

And if the action is necessary in the middle of the night or on a weekend, you must be prepared for an emergency visit to the veterinarian. *Before* this happens, know the address and phone number of the emergency veterinary coverage in your area and the amount of the initial fee required. Have that amount of money plus cab fare, if necessary, avail-

able in cash at all times. Simply put it in an enve-
lope marked "Kitty's Emergency Fund" and put it
away where you won't spend it. Add to it from time
to time. Realistically, it should contain a few hundred dollars unless you have good reserves to draw
on. And remember: no matter how much money
you have in the bank, most emergency services require cash or a particular credit card. Believe it or
not, in many cities animals die for lack of veterinary
care because their owners have not planned ahead.

"Fat on the Brain"—Obesity or Retardation?

The good news is that there is still one common
disease among cats that is noncontagious, treatable,
requires no vaccine, no medication, no expense.
OBESITY.

Most people-owned cats are obese. They may die
as the result of obesity—failure of one organ or
another which cannot sustain any stress because it
has been invaded by fat. A normal, enormous cat
weighs ten pounds. Average cats weigh from five to
eight. CATS SHOULD BE SVELTE.

I recall one cat owner who brought two cats into
the clinic in separate mesh-sided carriers. She stood
at the desk and demanded that her cats be checked
for "retardation." "Tell the vet they don't do nothing but sit around like blobs." "Blobs" indeed! Everyone in the room peered into the carriers and saw
exactly that. I told the woman the cats were not
retarded, just obese. One weighed eighteen pounds,
the other fifteen. Neither should have weighed even
eight.

On another occasion a prominent veterinarian's
distant cousin called — at his instance — for "be-

havioral advice." Her four-year-old male cat urinated
and defecated all over the house. I asked about health.
Seems the cat had a history of blockage and had
finally had surgery to create a new urinary tract
opening. Personality? Tough, irascible. How much
did he weigh? Twenty-two pounds! I couldn't imagine why he was still alive. However, I put him on a
diet of one tablespoon of Science Diet Feline Dry
Food a day plus 500 mg. of vitamin C twice a day,
to reduce weight to less than ten pounds; then increase to one-third cup a day of the same food. The
cousin was kind enough to report back that all housebreaking problems had ceased. Now, with a little
luck, the cat might survive to a reasonable age. Of
course, the cat owner, appalled at the diet, had
before embarking on it called the vet to check it out.
She was told to do *exactly* as told. And did.

Another cat owner called the clinic to make an
appointment to have a cat declawed. She happened
to comment that the cat was *very nasty*. How much
did the cat weigh? "I don't know—I can't lift her."
Finally, when told we would not take the appointment until she told us the weight, the owner weighed
the cat and reported back: twenty pounds (on a
female yet!). "And she doesn't eat much; I only feed
her one-half can in the morning and one-half can at
night and leave a little dish of dry food out all day."
Told that we would not accept the cat for surgery of
any kind, the woman became distraught but agreed
to put the cat on a diet. She may call us back when
the cat is down to ten or eleven pounds and still
losing, aiming at less than eight.

A mother in the Bronx made an appointment for
declaw of two cats to be picked up by us because
she couldn't leave the baby alone. As fate would

have it, I happened to accompany the driver that day and went in for the cats. Turned out they were being declawed because "they scratched the baby, but I love them too much to get rid of them." One was slightly overweight; the other was a nine-year-old seventeen-pound beauty who proceeded to shred the owner's arm upon being picked up to be put in the carrier. In this case, we took the cats because the owner explained they would be "put to sleep" otherwise and signed a waiver acknowledging the likelihood of the nine-year-old's death and that declaw was an "alternative to euthanasia." She promised to pick up the three bowls full of cat food (three kinds) sitting around the kitchen and put her cats on a rigid diet.

On another occasion a group of animal workers came to the clinic for a meeting, and one of them brought a cat she had rescued from the ASPCA where it ended up after being abandoned on the streets in the Bronx. The cat was magnificent and enormous—twenty-seven pounds, to be exact. Since she was an unspayed female and surgery was out of the question because of her weight, we volunteered to keep her until she lost weight. Mellen, as we named her, was with us for three months, during which we came to love her very much—and to reduce her weight to sixteen pounds. Unfortunately, however, she succumbed to a virus that in an adult cat would ordinarily respond to minimal treatment. One can only wish the person who fed her to death and abandoned her when she could hardly walk had been forced to spend that final week with her. It was gruesome.

I spend many hours every week talking to cat owners about the problems of cystitis, blockage, heart

disease, leukemia, anemia, gingivitis, and so forth.
But if I spend ten hours a week on these subjects
combined, I must spend twenty on the disease that
exacerbates all of the foregoing as well as every
other facet of a cat or cat owner's life: obesity and
overfeeding.

You should be able to see the feline silhouette.
There may rarely be coat hanging beneath the
abdomen, and there should not be flesh flapping
back and forth. If your cat is overweight, put him on
a diet. Please don't decide arbitrarily that your cat
couldn't be overweight because your vet never men-
tioned it. Unfortunately, fat cats have lots of health
problems that pay their veterinarians' mortgages.

Now, how can you weigh your cat? Simple. Stand
on the bathroom scale holding your cat. The reading
tells your combined weight. Put the cat down on the
floor, and then note your own weight. Subtract your
weight from the combined weight. You now have
your cat's weight. Please don't be like the client
who called to say, "I bought a baby scale but he
won't stand on it!" No, he won't. Particularly knowing there's a diet in the offing. . . .

And diet it is for a fat cat, or even a "plump" one.
One tablespoon of dry cat food daily. You will be
surprised at how long it takes for the weight to
come off. If you have more than one pet and some
are fat and some thin, you must feed the overweight
ones separately and limit their food intake severely.
Just put them in the bathroom with the food. Yes,
they will pester you for more food the first few
days, but they will get accustomed to the new regimen quite quickly and won't bother you *as long as
you don't respond*. If your cat seems particularly
hungry, give him a piece of raw vegetable. It's good

It's easy to see what to eliminate from this tom's diet.

for him. And if he doesn't eat it, you'll know he isn't really hungry!

Once they have lost weight, a normal male cat eats about one-third cup of dry food daily, a normal female cat about one-quarter cup. A cat who tends to put on weight easily or is very small should obviously be fed less. All normal cats (and dogs) are hungry all the time, so don't be swayed by the *cat's* idea of how much he eats. Just watch his figure and the scale.

Additionally, if you have an overweight cat, you should be aware that he will have many more health problems than a normal-weight cat (particularly cystitis and blockage). Furthermore, if surgery is necessary, the surgery itself will pose special, tedious, and even dangerous conditions because of the layers of fat to be cut through to reach the actual surgery site. Too, *fat* cats generally bleed excessively and heal slowly. They also present problems to the veterinarian with regard to anesthesia because the fat acts like a sponge, absorbing anesthesia so that it frequently takes more anesthesia per pound of body weight to anesthetize an obese animal and it takes longer for the cat to detoxify anesthesia following surgery. Vets quite properly impose added fees for surgery on obese pets.

You might also be interested to know that if you go to an emergency service with an obese pet, you may not be taken too promptly. The doctor's priority must be for the animals with the greatest chance of survival. Your fat cat doesn't fall into that category!

Your fat, *nasty* pet is an even greater disaster. Any vet with reasonable common sense handles a nasty animal only after completing all other necessary work. Then if the vet gets hurt badly, at least only the nasty one is left unattended. So don't expect all the care and solicitude in the world directed at you and your nasty, fat cat!

The Drug Scene

People do the strangest things: they drink too much; they take medicines they don't even need in quantities that are unthinkable if they think at all; they abuse drugs. Unfortunately, they also do all of these things with regard to their pets.

Luckily, cats are not as receptive as dogs to eating marijuana, hashish, cocaine. Nor are they much inclined to liquor. So usually people have to force it on them.

Before doing so, one should realize that the cat, a small animal by comparison with man, is generally very sensitive to drugs and medications and should not be given even the most minimal amounts of any drug except by veterinary prescription.

I particularly find that people who take painkillers or tranquilizers believe it's reasonable to give the same substances to their pets. It is *not*. They don't need them; you may kill them; you will, in any case, frighten and confuse them. It's very cruel.

Similarly, don't give even such common medications as aspirin and Valium. Cats cannot tolerate them. They also cannot tolerate many commonly available canine products, including flea and tick preparations made for dogs. Never use any product on a cat unless the label specifically states that it may be used for cats and indicates a dosage level.

DVMs and DVAs
Choosing a Veterinarian

Many years ago when ours was basically an agrarian society, people hardly every chose a veterinarian. There was probably one in the area; he had got into the field through interest, not financial motivation; and he lived pretty much the way everyone else in town did—poorly in poor communities; modestly in middle-income towns; and, on rare occasions, well in wealthier locales. He (rarely she) was part of the community. Most citizens owned animals for one reason or another. The vet's fortunes rose and fell with those of his neighbors, whose lives he shared.

By the second half of the twentieth century, however, the situation had changed radically. The raising of food animals was no longer a way of living; it had become a high-profit industry called factory farming, with vets completely its own. At the same time owning an animal as a pet came to be looked upon as a privilege of the middle and upper classes. The urban poor were prohibited from having pets in housing projects; so were the lower-middle class and the aged living in "created" communities. Laws restricting pet ownership to one or two animals per household began to appear on the books across the nation. All this was happening while the stray population reached astronomical proportions with humane euthanasia statistics soaring to an estimated 20 million pets a year in the late 1970s.

And where was the vet in all this? Viewing vet school as several times more difficult to get into than medical school and therefore deserving of an economic reward at least equal to that of a physician, if not more so. Not surprising that veterinary medicine became a prime money career by 1970. But also not surprising that with many pursuing it and fewer able to own pets, keen competition for the client and the dollar would soon follow.

And that's where we start today. Too many vets; too much money orientation; few clients able to pay the fees demanded of them for all-too-often mediocre, uninspired vet care. If you think I err, ask your vet to lend you a copy of the *Journal of the American Veterinary Medical Association* (why, in fact, isn't it in the reception room, where professional journals once were?). If your vet won't let you see it, go to the local library and read a few issues. Also, have a peek at *Veterinary Economics* magazine. If you thought the AMA lived in the Dark Ages, you have quite a surprise in store.

So choosing a vet these days is one of the hardest tasks a pet owner faces, particularly in a large city where anonymity protects the incompetent. If you live in a small community, you probably have heard from other pet owners how they feel about their vets: whether they answer emergencies, urge preventive care, keep up to date, charge fair prices ("less than a pediatrician" is a good yardstock), and so on. In a large city with a transient pet-owning population, there frequently are many incompetent and/or unethical veterinarians who thrive because of pet-owner ignorance and lack of word-of-mouth reputation.

So now let me tell you a few points on which to base your judgment either in hindsight or for the

future. Since this is a cat book, I will deal with cats
only, but you can apply the same sort of information to any other pet.

• Does the vet recommend inoculating the cat for
calici, panleukopenia, and rhinotracheitis twice, two
to four weeks apart, to begin with and thereafter at
least once a year?

• Does he advise rabies vaccination if the cat goes
outdoors anywhere except New York City (which is
rabies-free) but recommend strongly that the cat not
go out?

• Does he demand a feline-leukemia test on every
cat, suggesting isolation until the results are in? Is
he aware there is a successful treatment for this
disease? If not, is he responsive to the possibility?

• Is he interested in nutritional and vitamin
therapies—and preventive care in general? (I personally believe the future of veterinary medicine lies,
as does human medicine, in the nutritional—orthomolecular—approach to both prevention and care
and that those committed to "hard drugs" are going
to find themselves out of the running in but a few
years.)

• Does he demand that you spay a female cat early
(certainly by five to six months of age) and castrate
a male by six months?

• Does he tell you frankly that declaw is trivial
surgery, or does he make a big deal of it and charge
accordingly?

• Does he think ash content in food causes cystitis
and blockage in males? (It doesn't.)

• When he sees a twelve-pound cat who should
weigh eight pounds, does he make an issue of overweight or simply say, "Tommy certainly looks
healthy!"?

• If your cat has ear mites, does he sell you a bottle of medication for a few dollars with the manufacturer's label on it? Or has he covered it with his own label to make it look like an esoteric prescription to justify a high price? (Does the medication actually get rid of mites in three weeks?)

• Does he remind you to bring in a stool sample to be checked for parasites? If there are any, does he give you medication to administer, or does he hospitalize the cat and charge accordingly?

• If you ask about hairballs, does he tell you to comb and brush your cat, or does he recommend Vaseline™ or Petromalt™?

• Does he tell you to feed dry food to avoid needless dentistries and anesthesia?

• Does he board cats in the vet hospital, the same facility that treats sick cats?

• Is he willing to provide comprehensive price information for basic care by phone in advance of office visits?

Some vets aren't even willing to communicate the cost of the office visit/examination! And others—an even greater threat to the pet owner—spend hours romancing clients, conjuring up dire diseases out of thin air and bills of extraordinary substance. These really are accountants who did *not* miss their calling. Veterinary medicine is a gold mine for them. Typically, vaccinations and injections are charged for separately even if combined by the manufacturer. (We have seen a charge of thirty dollars for an inoculation that cost the vet under one dollar, including needle and syringe.) These same "DVAs" ("doctors of veterinary accountancy") can manage to find reason to hospitalize a pet for anything. And even situations genuinely requiring a few days' hospitalization can be stretched into weeks or months. These practices obviously presuppose that the pet owner can and *should* afford such costs. They also presuppose a great deal of pet owner gullibility and ignorance. All because many vets view pet ownership as a privilege and have little sympathy for those unable to afford high-cost care. (Specifically, providing low-cost vet care is contrary to the official position of the AVMA, which constantly provides "DVAs" with up-to-the-minute rationales for opposing and harassing low-cost vet facilities in their area.*)

Important, too, in choosing a vet is whether or not he respects your caring for your pet. Does he act as if owning a pet were some sort of aberration? Such an attitude in a vet may seem a strange contradiction to those of us who consider it natural to care for an animal and to pay our veterinary bills. But all too often we meet vets who might greet the presentation of another pet with "Well, isn't he handsome" or "Mistletoe? How did you come up with that name on the Fourth of July?" or even "Goodness, what a grungy old tom!" OR EVEN WITH SILENCE! But instead they say "Another cat?!" as if saying, "Another leper?!" Personal charm is not a criterion for veterinary competence, but rude callousness has its limits, and you needn't support it.

In the same category fall the vets who can't bear to touch the animal. These are pathologists who missed their calling.

*"The Board authorized the collection and cataloging of all available information on encroachment of nonprofit organizations into private veterinary practice. . . . Suggested strategies that could be used to prevent such infringement are being prepared by AVMA's legal counsel." *Journal of the American Veterinary Medical Association*, vol. 176, no. 10 (May 15, 1980), p. 962.

If all these words about choosing a veterinarian seem a bit (or extremely) harsh, please be assured they were meant to be exactly that. I can think of no other way to stop the great veterinary rip-off than to confirm what many pet owners already suspect.

You can become part of the solution by looking askance, developing greater knowledge, being willing to follow your own intuition (who knows your pet better than you?), and speaking out about veterinary practices in your community. Now that there is the beginning of an excess of vets, we have the hope of raising the standards of the profession by openly boycotting its dregs. If you don't like what you see, say so and go elsewhere. Eventually, you'll find a good vet. They do exist!

"Linguine on Sundays?" *Diet*

A charming young Italian who still had a great deal of difficulty with our language brought in a six-month-old shiny black male cat for neutering; he was delighted to talk about his pet and acquire a vocabulary regarding the care of cats. All was perfect!

Six months later the same gentleman, no less charming and much more fluent in English, brought the same cat back to have him declawed. The cat hissed, clawed, and bit, and it took several technicians a great deal of time just to get him out of his carrier. After he was anesthetized, we learned he now weighed fourteen pounds—a cat who should weigh eight pounds! When I explained the situation to the owner—who would have to remove his pet's bandages himself since we couldn't get near the cat without reanesthetizing—he wrote down all the diet information in great detail. Then he asked whether the cat could still continue to have linguine with white clam sauce—his favorite—"just on Sunday, maybe? He loves pasta."

So I really feel like starting by saying that most cats should be on a diet. But I content myself first with telling you what they should eat and why—and then how much.

The section on kittens (page 61) addresses itself to feeding. So I trust you will follow that advice if you have young ones.

It is very important that you understand the need for your adult cat to eat the same food, same quantity, every day. You might consider that approach dull, but your cat won't.

You see, the only way to know whether a cat is sick, given that he can't talk, is by his patterns of eating, drinking, urinating, defecating. The first signs of a problem are loss of appetite, drinking more or less water than usual, blood in the urine, inability to urinate, constipation, or diarrhea. Cats who eat proper diets—the same thing in the same quantity day in, day out—are much easier to judge than those who eat today, turn down food tomorrow, have fish one day, liver the next, and so on. Usually if such cats don't eat, their owners figure they simply don't like the giblet stew and are holding out for filet mignon.

So that you will understand *why* to feed *what*, let's review the types of food.

Canned foods are usually 80 percent or more moisture. Some brands are balanced; many are not.

Canned food provides nothing for the cat to chew, smells awful, gives many cats diarrhea, costs a lot, and is heavy to carry home from the store. The only purpose I can see for it is something in which— when necessary—to mix medications, vitamins, and so forth, or to use in tempting a very sick cat who has lost his appetite. (Usually mackerel will do nicely. Whatever you do, avoid tuna; it creates a condition called steatitis, with which there is an enormous fatty buildup on the cat's breastbone, which *kills*.)

Soft-moist food comes in little packages of semi-

Jasmine, who ate one-half teaspoon of Mega C Plus vitamin supplement mixed in canned food, along with her Science Diet dry food, devotes her attention to polishing the inside of the empty can.

dried, semimoist morsels. These are usually heavily dyed (for your benefit, since Kitty doesn't see colors), heavily preserved, and they may contain sugar. They offer nothing hard for the cat to chew, create enormous amount of fecal matter, make Kitty use his litter constantly and you change it accordingly. Get off the dye and all the junk that goes with it!

Dry foods offer a high amount of nutrition in a small space at a low cost. These are an absolute necessity for keeping Kitty's teeth and gums in good condition. (Cats who do not eat dry food will require frequent dentistries or will die when their teeth and gums have deteriorated and they are unable to eat.) Try to avoid heavily dyed products, which are usually also the higher-bulk products. There are now cat foods on sale at feed dealers which have no dye and offer high-calorie, quality nutritional values and low bulk (like Science Diet Feline Dry Food, which all our cats eat exclusively). Do not be led into thinking you must also look for a natural, no-preservatives food. Pet foods usually sit around for a long time from manufacture to sale to use, and preservatives are still often a necessity. Always leave plenty of water available. Yes, cats *do* drink water, contrary to all those old tales.

The amount of lead in many pet foods has become a very major cause for concern. By-products such as bone meal and organ meat, produced in the United States, are said to be sold exclusively for use in pet food because their lead levels are too high for *human* consumption. The result: your eight-pound cat may consume enough lead in a year to prove toxic to a two-year-old child. Veterinarians have for some years found low-level anemia a complicating factor in many diseases but did not realize its source

Some of the author's cats at breakfast.

(anemia is a symptom of lead poisoning). We now know that the pet's diet may provide the answer,* and we must in the future force cat food manufacturers to get lead levels under control. The best advice we can offer right now is to stay away from products specifically containing the organ meats kidney and liver. Also avoid bone meal, if possible—it's very difficult. And write pet food manufacturers requesting information on lead levels in their food and making clear that high levels are unacceptable.

*See "Lead in Animal Foods" by James G. Fox, DVM, MS; Franklin D. Aldrich; and George W. Boylen, Jr., BS, in *Journal of Toxicology and Environmental Health*, 1:461–67, 1976, copyright 1976 Hemisphere Publishing Corporation; and "Analysis of Lead in Animal Feed Ingredients," by James G. Fox, DVM, MS; and George W. Boylen, Jr., BS; in *American Journal of Veterinary Research*, vol. 39, no. 1, copyright 1978 by American Veterinary Medical Association. The authors of these two articles are affiliated with the Division of Laboratory Animal Medicine and Environmental Medical Service, Medical Department, Massachusetts Institute of Technology, Cambridge, Mass. Requests for reprints should be sent to James G. Fox, DVM, MS, Animal Care Facility, 20C-133, Massachusetts Institute of Technology, Cambridge, Mass. 02139.

We are unable to give you the names of the products to stay away from because the researchers at MIT who have the information advise they are not permitted to release it. It may interest you to know, however, that vitamin C acts to detoxify lead, so the cats receiving vitamin C have a great advantage.

Those of you who follow vegetarian diets yourself should not impose such a diet on your cats. It will contain insufficient or no taurine (a product of animal protein) and result in blindness. For the same reason, dog food, with its lower protein level, is insufficient for cats.

Needless to say, my own cats eat 100 percent dry food: specifically, Science Diet Feline Dry Food. No, the males do not suffer from blockages; no, they don't refuse to eat it (healthy cats do not starve themselves); no, they don't need a change; no, ash content is not relevant (it's very high in canned foods if you subtract the moisture percentage and recalculate the percentage of ash in the substance of the food, so obviously, it's not the answer to anything).

Since I use both vitamin C and Brewers Yeast with the dry food, I can suggest an easy way to feed to be sure the supplements are eaten. Put the dry food in the dish first. Spray water from a plant mister very gently over the top of the food and then sprinkle the powdered Mega C Plus or vitamin C (ascorbic acid crystals) over the food and similarly the Brewers Yeast. The supplements will stick to the food and be eaten readily. I do suggest you start with the minimal amount of each supplement and work up to a daily dosage of approximately 750–1,000 mg. of vitamin C and ½ teaspoon of Brewers Yeast per cat. Brewers Yeast can be purchased from your local health food store. Ascorbic acid crystals (powder)

Matilda, sitting under a heat lamp, cleans her paws after breakfast. Well beyond 15 years old, she's a healthy, happy cat.

can be purchased at low cost by writing Bronson Pharmaceuticals, 4526 Rinetti Lane. La Canada. Calif. 91011 (213–790–2646).

Now, QUANTITY. First, know that all normal healthy cats are hungry all the time. A large adult neutered cat generally eats one-third cup of dry cat food a day, once a day in the morning, please. That's all! And if the cat does not eat *that* quantity within fifteen minutes, pick up the remainder and feed even less the next day. I know the package tells you to feed more, but the manufacturer is selling cat food.

The largest cat we have ever seen at its correct weight weighed under eleven pounds. Most cats weigh from five to eight pounds. Some perfectly

normal cats weigh under five pounds. Clearly, they
need considerably less than one-third cup of food
daily.

If you have a houseful of cats weighing over eight
pounds, get them on a diet immediately. Those who
are immensely fat can be put on one tablespoon of
food a day. You will be surprised at how long it
takes for them to lose any meaningful amount of
weight—months!

Your cats will do a lot of carrying on to begin
with, but once they sense your determination, they
will calm down. You will like the effect of the diet
once everyone settles into it. You will find them
more playful, more fun, better-natured, younger in
attitude and looks. You should not be able to tell
your ten-year-olds from your two-year-olds.

You will also find when diets are correct that you
need to change litter much less often and your cats
present no housebreaking problems. By contrast
overfed cats are very sloppy about housebreaking
and are lazy and dull in general.

So with proper diet your cats improve in looks,
health, and disposition, and you save time and
money.

Male Cats and Urinary Tract Problems

Are you wondering whether you can apply this
diet information to your male cat who has a history
of blockage, has eaten only canned food for years,
and once again needs dental work? The last time his
teeth were worked on, it took him several days to
recover from the anesthesia. You're not looking forward to that risk again. "Dry food," you say to
yourself, "would be a blessing if only we could . . ."

Ivy knows where the food is.

I have several male cats who were "dumped" at the clinic with cystitis or blockage or both. They were started on canned food and given 500 mg. of vitamin C three or four times daily. Over a period of a month, each was switched to Science Diet Feline Dry Food. The vitamin C continued as previously and gradually was decreased to twice a day. Then we discovered the benefits of Mega C Plus (see page 25) for treating feline leukemia and noticed that

none of the many male cats in the leukemia program ever developed cystitis or blockage and tha
all the females with a lengthy history of cystitis
ceased to be troubled with the condition. Cats who
chronically formed bladder stones also ceased to do
so.

Therefore, we switched all cystitis/blockage-prone
males to one teaspoon Mega C Plus powder in thei
usual morning meal and one 500-mg. vitamin C
tablet in the evening. No difficulties were encountered
Next, the evening vitamin C tablets were eliminated
All went well and continues that way after two
years of this regimen. Obviously, the ascorbic acid
crystals I use with my own cats (page 56) are equally
satisfactory.

It is our conclusion, as many veterinarians believe
that much cystitis and blockage are related to insufficient acidity of the urine and also to the inability
of the cat's body to control or eliminate viruses
present in the urinary tract, where they contribute
to or cause cystitis and blockage. Obviously, if cystitis and blockage can be controlled or prevented by
keeping cats thin and active, and by providing vitamin C therapy, then dry food, ash content, and a
narrow, funnel-shaped urethra are not causes of
urinary-tract problems in male cats.

Bladder Stones and Impacted Intestines

Those of us who have many cats inevitably get
one who not only forms bladder stones, suffers a
good deal of pain, and frequently urinates blood
but also has extreme difficulty defecating. The stone
formation problem is usually treated somewhat un-

successfully with a variety of drugs, and the intestinal condition is usually treated by feeding canned cat food or baby food mixed with Siblin℗ or a similar human-oriented dietary additive laxative. Everyone with a cat like this knows only too well the unpleasantness all this entails for both cat and human. Pain and discomfort continue to some degree throughout the cat's life, and of course the owner cleans up the frequent messes. The situation is made doubly distasteful by the fact that the cat—as a result of the frequent discomfort—is irascible and downright unappreciative!

My cat in this category is Matilda, a stunning golden split-face tortoiseshell *well* along in years when she adopted me by biting me while I was conducting a tour of her shelter room at a humane institution. Our antagonistic relationship endured eight years of medication and mess. Now Matilda's daily diet consists of one-quarter cup Science Diet Feline Dry Food plus two tablespoons of canned food containing at least one teaspoon of ascorbic acid crystals. Stones, bloody urine, total constipation, all have ceased. So have growling and biting. We have a new problem though: Matilda tries to sleep, purring, on my head every night.

Kittengarten

By the time you get halfway through this section, you might think it's easier to have a baby.

Kittens are lots of fun. They're cute. They're cuddly. They are little monsters. They will eat your plants, chew electric wires and electrocute themselves, crawl into the funniest places and not be able to get out, forget to eat and get very weak, decide to play at three in the morning. . . .

But they can be a lot easier to live with if you expect all these things and get organized.

First, food. At this point most kittens may eat whatever quantities they desire. For a four- to six-week-old kitten, buy some totally dry kitten food (or lacking that, dry cat food). Add a bit of hot water and cottage cheese. An alternative is to add infant formula to the dry food. If the kitten is four to six weeks of age, the mixture must be wet enough for the kitten to lap up. She will not bite into food and scoop up mouthfuls at that age. As the food dries and becomes less liquid, add water. Kittens rarely drink water alone, so they need it in the food, as well as needing it in order to be able to eat the food. As the days pass, gradually use less water in the food. But make sure there is always a dish of water on the side. By ten weeks of age, the kitten should be eating slightly moistened kitten food and cottage cheese, and by four months of age or less, she should be eating dry cat food.

Many kittens do not eat when first taken away from their brothers and sisters. They forget. They don't know how. They lack the competition of the others to make them eat. If this seems to be your kitten's situation, put food on the kitten's nose, in her mouth if necessary. Immediately thereafter put her head gently into the food dish so she knows where the food comes from. You may have to open the kitten's mouth by pinching the corners lightly and force-feed her. It is absolutely imperative that the kitten eat enough to maintain her weight and then grow. She does not have to get fat, however, as many think.

If you happen to acquire a very young kitten who has not been weaned (taught to eat other than nursing) at all, you might teach her by using a mixture of baby food, infant formula, and a tiny amount of powdered (blenderized) kitten food. *But heed this warning*: feeding baby food and formula to a great degree for too long a period (more than a few days) will give the kitten diarrhea, which can be fatal. Put the mixture into the corner of the kitten's mouth by using a demitasse spoon or syringe. Let the kitten learn to swallow naturally. As the meals go by, mix in more and more powdered kitten food. Feed a three- to five-week-old kitten four or five times a day minimum. After that point once she starts eating on her own, three feedings or food left available will suffice.

We also start all our kittens on Mega C Plus powder (instructions are on the container) so as to prevent feline leukemia and other diseases, notably respiratory conditions, and recommend you do likewise. Ascorbic acid crystals may be substituted, using ⅛ teaspoon (4 grams to the teaspoon) a day per kitten. We also use ¼ teaspoon Brewers Yeast daily.

Your kitten must be kept warm. Prepare a small room in which the temperature is kept at least 68° F (20° C). Put into the room a box containing a small towel or cloth that the kitten can use as a bed. Be sure this box is in a draft-free area. Also put in the room a small litter tray with a minimal amount of litter just barely covering the bottom. The room should have no electric wires the kitten can chew on, no plants, nothing else harmful. Assume the kitten will chew or play with everything available, and act accordingly. The kitten may sleep in bed with you if your bedroom is safe, but check conditions carefully. It is tragic for the kitten to find some fatal plaything while you are sleeping.

If there is any doubt about the warmth of the room, use a hot-water bottle or heating pad in the kitten's bed. If you use a heating pad, tape the wires under something, out of the kitten's reach. Heat lamps, used cautiously, are also recommended.

I believe that many young kittens do not do well without another kitten or cat and personally hesitate to let a kitten go to a catless home. So if you are adopting a kitten, consider two. They will be no more work than one, and they'll keep each other happy and healthy.

Kittens need veterinary care as described in the "Feline Health" section earlier in this chapter. But I would particularly remind you here that worms and coccidia are common and should be checked for regularly by taking a stool sample to your vet. Ear mites also present problems and should be watched for—black crumbly material in the ears or scratching at the ears, rubbing of the head.

Declaw is best done at twelve weeks of age. Spay may be done at the same time on the same anesthesia. Castration should be done at six months. Stick with this timetable if you're starting with young kittens. Time passes quickly if you have not calendared your kittens' needs. Do so now.

The Handicapped Cat, Whatever That Is

This title derives from the fact that my so-called "handicapped" pets have never demonstrated any overwhelming problems and have in many instances proved that they can be just as obnoxious as anyone else.

Blind cats and dogs have no difficulty, provided you don't move all the furniture every day. I must say the cats do better than the dogs and those blind from birth do better than those losing their sight later on. In particular, my blind street cat (picked up at six months of age in a construction site in the midst of the East River Drive) is the toughest cat I have. He was born blind with congenital cataracts; both eyes have now been removed because of glaucoma. None of which has deterred him in the least. One amusing note: he has obviously learned that when he hears the light switch turned off, the other cats are at a momentary disadvantage while their eyes adjust. It is at this very second that he will attack another cat. I have dealt with this situation by warning him not to attack anyone as I turn out the light. Also, I note the other cats all watch him as I reach for the switch. No dummies there.

If you have a blind cat, be aware that many causes of blindness will also result in glaucoma. If you see any increase in size of the eye, you may as well ask your veterinarian to remove (enucleate) it immediately. Glaucoma is painful, and it is hardly worth treating an already visionless eye.

Deaf cats are no problem at all, except that they can't hear you (they may be lucky). They will learn quickly enough to follow your hand motions, and may, like my deaf dog, learn to lip-read.

Lameness or lack of a limb is meaningless to animals. My fastest-moving cat has four legs and three feet, probably from birth. He is named Flash because he always flashes by. His motto is "Don't

walk, run!" Unfortunately, he has not grown wings
yet, but he is still hopeful.

"She Can't Be Pregnant—
He's Her Brother!"
Anatomy I

Cats have long presented a very sensual image to
mankind. But beyond that we generally know very
little about their sexuality. What we do know has
often been learned the hard way: the queen who
gave birth in the bottom of the closet one night
three months after you named her George; the tom
who started spraying your living room, even though
his name was Serena.

Every day we hear many hilarious stories in a
spay/neuter clinic that sees a couple hundred cats a
week. So many stories and questions, in fact, that
we often refer to these conversations as "Anatomy
I."

So let's talk straight facts.

Female cats can come into season (what some call
"in heat") by four months of age, usually before six
months. They can be impregnated from this point
on at any fertile moment. What is most deceptive
for many owners is that the cat appears to go in and
out of season from one day to the next, sometimes
seeming to be in season for a week, out for a week,
in for three days, out for four days, and so on.
Actually, the hormone level in the cat's body changes
little. During the spaying operations, we notice that
almost every female cat seems to be in season from

February through October. From November through
January about 60 percent of the adult female cats
are in season at the moment of surgery. So obviously they are not out of season for very long, and
that infertile period is not to be relied upon.

When in season, many female cats yowl, rub
against you and everything else in sight, try to get
out any available window or door, urinate all over
the house, literally scream twenty-four hours a day,
roll on the floor, walk around with back arched and
tail aloft. Some show no signs whatsoever, being in
what is called "silent season." Obviously, "silent
seasons" are most deceptive and no more to be
relied upon than the short infertile periods.

And don't think your cat won't get pregnant because she's living with her brother, father, son,
cousin, or whatever. Such niceties are meaningless
among animals (and some humans, you may recall).
Also, don't think she won't get pregnant because
they don't *seem* interested in one another, or because they seem like such babies to you. Nature
takes its course. . . .

Female cats, whether they are nursing or not,
usually come into season and get pregnant (if there
is a male present) six to eight weeks after the birth
of a litter. Do not believe that cats do not get pregnant while nursing. They certainly do, as too many
people have found out the hard way.

Cats may be spayed easily while in season, while
having milk in their breasts, while pregnant (in which
case it's an abortion/spay). In fact, almost every cat
we spay at the clinic falls into one of these catego-
ries or one of the following. (When we started building a collection of normal and abnormal uteruses
and ovaries for educational purposes, we had an

Rear of female cat.
Space between rectum and
genitals is less than
on male cat.

Rear of a male cat.

example of almost every "abnormality" within a week. But it took more than two weeks to find a "normal" uterus and ovaries.)

Pyometras. Unspayed female cats as they grow older often develop a condition called pyometra, in which the horns of the uterus fill with pus. The situation reaches a point where the abdomen is extremely distended, as in pregnancy, and there is a great deal of infection. The cat must be spayed, treated with antibiotics by the veterinarian, and usually discharged with antibiotics for home use. Pyometra is a life-threatening situation, its symptoms generally unnoticed by the owner until the cat has reached the point of severe infection. Then she no longer eats, drinks, or moves about. There may or may not be an elevated temperature (normal again is 101.5° F, or 38.6° C). We are told pyometra occurs most frequently in the unspayed cat over four years of age. At the clinic, however, we have seen pyometras in cats as young as six months—cats brought in bleeding (generally misdiagnosed as cystitis), not eating, becoming listless. It cannot be stressed too strongly that this condition is immediately life-threatening; the cat must be spayed, treated properly, and receive correct aftercare at home . . . specifically, she must not be allowed to become constipated, refusing food and water; she must be urinating and defecating in order to clear her body of both the anesthetic and the infection. Her body temperature must be monitored twice daily; high-quality food must be provided. Otherwise, there will be a dead cat. I often think "pyometra" is nature's "instant karma" for those who say, "It's not natural to spay."

Unspayed cats also develop mammary tumors, often malignant. That is, they are likely to develop cancer if left unspayed and if surviving the likelihood of pyometra and such.

Ovarian Cysts. Unspayed cats with a high level of hormone activity form cysts on the ovaries and uterus. These conditions are often found in cats described by their owners as "constantly in heat" or "screaming" all the time when in heat—the cats who keep people awake at night. We commonly see these conditions in cats as young as seven months. Cats with these conditions could scarcely be "comfortable."

Friable Uterus. Then there's the friable uterus, or uterus and ovaries. Friable indicates a situation in which, probably as a result of hormone activity or multiple pregnancies, the uterus is fragile, breaking, tearing, shredding. It often splits as the veterinarian removes it, necessitating additional surgery time. Vets gripe a lot about friable uteruses—with reason.

Mucometras. Also, we see mucometras. In this case the uterus has filled with mucus. It is enlarged as in a pyometra, making the cat uncomfortable and unhealthy. Mucometra is probably a result of hormone imbalance and can develop into pyometra. Basically, all previous comments about pyometra pertain to mucometra as well.

If you have a cat spayed and are told by the veterinarian that she was in season or had any of the conditions described above, it is significant that you realize what experience has shown: She will still attract males for a minimuum of five days after spaying, she may be receptive to breeding, and if she is bred, she may get a very severe (read "fatal") infection. She must be prevented from getting bred—kept away from male cats.

Are you wondering at this point what creates all of the conditions just described? Hormone activity provides an environment in which malignancies and infections of the reproductive organs thrive. If your cat is not spayed and is over five months of age, you are sitting there waiting for her to develop one life-threatening condition or another—to say nothing of the discomfort she suffers when in season. And no, breeding will not prevent these conditions. So pick up the phone and make an appointment with your vet or low-cost spay/neuter clinic immediately.

And what is the spay operation for which you are making an appointment? It is an ovariohysterectomy. To be specific: the female cat is given injectible, general anesthesia. The bladder is expressed (emptied). The abdominal area is shaved and scrubbed with a sterilizing solution. The cat is then secured on the surgery table and the surgery site draped. The surgeon makes a small (usually about an inch) incision in the abdomen and inserts the spay hook (resembling an oversized crochet hook). Using this hook, the uterus and ovaries are lifted out through the incision, clamped off with hemostats, and ligated (tied off) with sutures or a sterile metal clip. They are then severed with a scalpel blade and removed and the stumps dropped back into the abdominal cavity. The incision is then sutured closed. At Pet Clinicare animals are tattooed with an "S" after spay so that they may be identified as neutered pets in the future. As such they will not be destroyed automatically should they wind up in a shelter.

The surgery takes about ten minutes. The cat should be returned to the owner the following day with a few sutures, no bandages, no bleeding, and no discomfort. Inactivity or withdrawn behavior on the cat's part at this point is due to anesthesia and often is the result of constipation from her having fasted for some hours before surgery as well as being inactive the day of surgery. Do not attribute her inactivity or withdrawn behavior to the surgery and fail to treat it appropriately. Use a large dab of Vaseline™ on her nose as a laxative (she will lick it off), and make sure she is urinating and defecating, then eating and drinking normally within forty-eight hours of her return home. You must even force-feed if necessary for a day or so. The sutures will be removed by your veterinarian approximately ten days after surgery.

Now what about male cats?

Well, you certainly know a lot more about them— particularly the day your male cat suddenly realizes he is male and "sprays" (urinates) all over your house. You walk in from work and are greeted by an odor not to be described. Then you know all about male cats!

The male cat's testicles generally descend and become obvious under his tail when he is about four to five months of age. He is not mature enough for neutering until around six months, unless he has reached the point of spraying before then. Any male cat old enough to spray is old enough to be castrated—"neutered," "fixed," "altered."

When a male cat is neutered, he is first given a general, injectible anesthesia. The scrotum is then shaved and cleaned with alcohol preparatory to surgery. An incision is made in the scrotum and each testicle is freed and lifted out. The blood vessels to the testicles are ligated (tied off) and the testicles snipped off. It is very simple, external process requiring two to three minutes' veterinary time. Usually when the cat returns to you, he may have a bit of dried blood on the scrotum, occasionally even some fresh bleeding. Most cats will clean themselves, and there certainly is nothing for you to clean up or worry about. Let nature take its course. There are no sutures to be removed in a normal external castration.

Occasionally a cat's testicles do not descend normally; one or both may be retained within the body. It is absolutely necessary that the retained

testicle or testicles be removed surgically to prevent
the growth of tumors associated with the undescended testicles as well as to render the cat sterile.
Removal of undescended testicles will often result
in a few sutures to be removed ten days after surgery.

Experience has shown that a male cat may not
cease to be male until three to four weeks after
neutering. So please be aware that he should not be
left with unspayed adult females. Not only can he
breed and impregnate them, but (as has been ob-
served in several cases) he can breed them repeatedly,
to the point of dying. So don't bring him home from
the hospital and leave him with an unspayed female.

All cats return home from the hospital carrying
the odors picked up there. Other cats at home will
become antagonistic, ignoring the returned cat or
attacking him, often rolling him over and around to
put the scent of the house back on him. Don't be
alarmed at this behavior. It will pass quickly enough
as the cat reacquires the scent of the house and is
once again integrated into the "pet pack."

There is no information in this book on breeding
cats since it will be at least the year 2000 before
there will be any need to make an effort to breed
cats. By then I'll update the book. It would be a
pleasure to have to add a breeding section because
the streets were no longer full of starving, homeless
cats.

Sandpaper Houses for Cats Who Can't Scratch Themselves

Declaw (Permanent Removal of All Claws)

When I was first adopted by two cats, I fortunately had no contact with those people who tell all the strange stories about declawing cats. I simply took the cats to my vet for "the works"—including declaw, all four feet. I picked them up forty-eight hours later. And they were just the same cats.

As I was adopted by more cats, I did the same. I never thought anything about it since my cats do all the normal cat things. But they don't destroy anything, and they don't harm the dogs or each other. They also are easy to bathe, brush, medicate if ill, and so forth. Who knew about all the craziness on the subject?

When we opened the spay/neuter clinic, I added declaw as a service. I knew it should be done on the same anesthesia as the neutering (no, it doesn't require more or longer anesthesia) and because it was my repeated experience when working as a volunteer at the ASPCA that most cats were abandoned by their owners or permitted to roam because they scratched everything to bits—furniture, children, dogs. I believed if people could have their cats declawed cheaply ($15 or $25), most would do so and keep their cats.

Time has proved that assumption very accurate. It has also proved that most cat owners will acquire *many* more cats (taking them off the streets) if they can neuter and declaw cheaply. So on any given day, one-half to two-thirds of the cats the clinic sees will be declawed and live happily every after in the comfort of someone's home rather than scurrying about the streets in fear and starvation. (Our average client has more than five cats.)

As my reward for the cat's having arrived at this comfortable life, I must live with insults and death threats from people who believe and add to all the nonsense about declaw. The one cheerful note at this point is that the clinics that have opened since Pet Clinicare also offer declaw. . . .

First let's dispense with all the ignorance and downright maliciousness; later we will talk about the actual mechanics of declaw.

Nonsense #1: "Declawed cats can't scratch them-selves." Obviously, if cats used their claws to scratch themselves, they would shred their skin, which they don't (unless ear mites or fleas are driving them mad; in that case, you don't want them able to shred their skin and create abcesses).

Nonsense #2: "They can't jump." Oh, I wish this were true. I would give anything to have my cats stay within even six feet of the floor.

Nonsense #3: "They lose their sense of balance." Really? Do you lose your sense of balance every time you crack and lose a nail? Hardly.

Nonsense #4: "They don't have the pleasure of scratching." I wish, I wish! If they knew their claws were missing and didn't scratch, I wouldn't have to replace the rolled edge on my sofa every few months. Nor would I be awakened by the sound of Cleo scratching (she thinks) the front of my desk. Declawed cats will scratch and enjoy forever.

Nonsense #5: "Declawed cats bite." As if cats with claws don't bite! If a cat is more dominant than its person, it will claw, bite, push, or do anything else it pleases. It does not do one as the result of not doing another. On the other hand, if Kitty is trying to dominate you to force you to dominate him and you do not respond to one means, he will undoubtedly try another until you exercise the authority he requires.

In this vein, I would repeat the sickest story I have heard to date. A woman called two days after her cat was declawed, crying because he couldn't scratch her. When I said I could not figure out what she was talking about, she continued, in tears: "Every morning he used to bite and scratch me. Well, this morning, he bit me but he couldn't scratch me. I feel so sorry for him because he enjoyed biting and scratching me!" (Wonder what her husband's pleasure is. . . .)

Nonsense #6: "Declawed cats can't protect themselves from dogs and other animals intent upon killing them." The nonsense here is that the cat should need to protect himself or could do so. Claws do not offer adequate protection from dogs or others intent upon killing, as those of us who have seen a cat killed by a dog or other animal can tell you. Claws also do not offer protection from cars and disease, which are the real threats out there in the world. It is the responsibility of the cat's owner to keep him safe from threats of all kinds—which means to keep him indoors at all times. Certainly, a cat should never have to live in a house with dogs who pose a threat to him. You kid yourself if you think a cat with claws will be all right with an aggressive dog. And while you're kidding yourself, you may be killing your cat.

Nonsense #7: "Declawed cats don't knead." If this were true, I would get ever so many more hours sleep! But it isn't, so every night I must deal with s-0all these kneading cats before getting the respite that allows me to fall asleep; in other words, after they finally go to sleep or, lacking that, are forcibly removed from my back, shoulders, and stomach, I can sleep.

Nonsense #8: "A cat's personality changes when it is declawed." Since declawing involves no chemical changes in the body, *how* could anyone believe this? What will change is the relationship between human and cat, since it's easier to get close—mentally and physically—to a cat with no claws. Your increased friendliness will result in a friendlier cat.

Nonsense # 9: "Declawed cats can't catch mice." So what are all those little decapitated things Tino brings me?

Then there are the physical-description-of-the-process irrationalities:

Stupidity #1: "The nails are pulled out." Actually, they are cut with the same clipper many people use to cut cats' nails but are cut back to the point where they don't regrow. (Somehow I could never visualize a veterinarian with a pair of pliers pulling out nails all day.)

Stupidity #2: "The cat can't walk for days or weeks." What may keep a cat down is anesthesia, not surgery. A twelve-week-old kitten will be up and moving a few hours after surgery; a fat ten-year-old may not feel like it for a day or two, but it's anesthesia and fat—not declaw—that slows him down for a day or two.

Stupidity #3: "They wake up wondering why their claws are missing." Perhaps these same ignorant people think cats also wake up missing their ovaries, uteruses, testicles, rotten teeth, ear mites, abcesses, and all the other things removed or treated while the cat is anesthesized.

Stupidity #4: "Claws are apt to regrow." They are not apt to regrow. Failure to remove all of the unguicular crest may result in a claw regrowth. But one hardly expects a competent vet to do incomplete declaws any more than he or she should be doing other incomplete surgery. A few animals can supposedly regrow practically anything (like female cats who are said to have regrown ovarian tissue); however, what regrows in these rare cases is simply removed with the ease of removing a hangnail. What owners believe to be regrown claws usually turn out to be calluses or scabs. As one whose tonsils seem to have regrown several times, however, I can surely confirm that regrowths can happen, are rare, and are not a matter of concern.

I will add just one wonderfully funny story. A very elderly woman called the clinic one day to make an appointment to have a stray cat neutered in the hope of finding him a home. We talked about vaccinations, feline leukemia test, and so on. Then she happened to say, "The only reason I'm not declawing him is it's so hard to find someone who'll put up the sandpaper." I think I said "I beg your pardon" twice. Then I asked, "What sandpaper?"

She then explained that she'd been told a declawed cat can't grip a surface and move about without having everything covered with sandpaper. "And it's so hard to find someone to adopt a cat who will bother covering the floors, furniture, draperies, and so forth, with sandpaper. . . ."

In the same vein, there's a pamphlet circulated by a so-called humane organization urging people not to declaw cats and citing all their "reasons." The diagram of a cat's claw included in the material is upside-down. The rest of the pamphlet is equally inaccurate.

All this could be hilarious if it had not resulted in the abandonment and/or death of millions of cats each year. . . . "I'd rather see him dead than declawed."

Hypocritical humane organizations that do little or nothing for animals raise additional millions each year with another "cruelty" to take a stand on. Millions of cat owners are ripped off each year for high veterinary charges for declaw. They enter a vet's office with tremendous guilts and doubts, the perfect victims for astronomically high bills for a simple, completely external procedure that takes less than five minutes of veterinary time. Instead of picking up their cats the next day, they leave them for three to five days (paying "hospitalization" fees, of course) rather than risk the possibility of seeing any signs of the declaw.

If only they knew!

First, let's understand the mechanics of it. Each digit of the cat's paw is composed of three phalanges. The claw or nail grows from the unguicular crest of the third phalanx. The digital pad lies under the second interphalangeal joint.

For the declawing procedure the cat is put under general (injectible) anesthesia, given an injection of antibiotic, and has its paws cleaned with alcohol. A tourniquet is placed on the leg. A guillotine-type nail clipper is used. The surgeon flexes the joint and positions the clipper so as to remove the third phalanx while avoiding the digital pad.

Pressure bandages are placed on the paws. Then the cat is put in a cage to sleep off the anesthesia, or other surgery (spaying, for example) is performed while the anesthesia is in effect. Within eight to twelve hours after surgery, the bandages are slipped off. Most cats have no bleeding at this point, only minimal spotting, and can go home with no discomfort to themselves and no inconvenience to their owners.

Some cats—usually old or vastly overweight or Siamese—bleed a good deal for a few minutes after the bandages are removed. If they are left undisturbed in their cages on absorbent paper for half an hour or so, the bleeding stops, and they may be discharged with everyone else.

The important thing for an owner to understand is that it is normal for a cat's paws to spot or even bleed at times during the few days immediately after surgery because the cat—feeling nothing to deter him—will walk, scratch, jump, dig in plants if permitted, and in general pursue all his normal activities. Some of these actions obviously will irritate his feet and cause some bleeding. We therefore recommend that the cat be confined for a couple of days in a "safe" (nonirritating) room like a bathroom. Or, if bleeding occurs, confine him immediately so that he is quiet and the bleeding stops. Then you continue from there a little more cautiously and wisely.

It is also necessary that shredded paper (toilet paper or newspaper) be substituted for litter for the

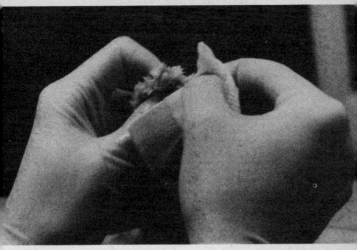

Paw of anesthetized cat is cleaned with alcohol preparatory to declaw.

Tourniquets on legs of cat preparatory to declaw.

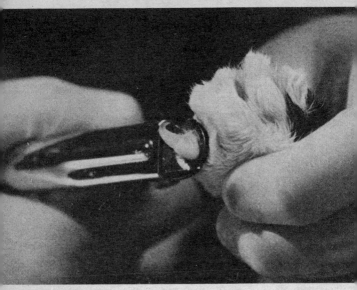

Using guillotine-type nail clipper, the veterinarian removes the claw and third phalanx.

first week to ten days after declaw, the period of time to be determined by the cat's age and therefore healing powers. If he's reluctant to use the paper in his box, put a tiny amount of litter under the paper to attract him. Most cats do not take immediately to the shredded paper in the litter box, so leave Kitty confined with it until he is indeed using it. The alternative being you-know-what all over the house.

Because declaw surgery requires anesthesia, you need to realize that the effects of anesthesia must be dealt with when the cat comes home. Many cats become constipated as a result of fasting before surgery combined with anesthesia. So it is recommended that you feed the cat a large dab of Vaseline™ upon

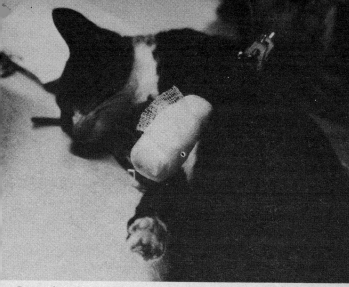

Gauze bandage is wrapped around each paw after declaw.

Porous tape is wrapped over gauze. The tabs will allow easy removal of bandages.

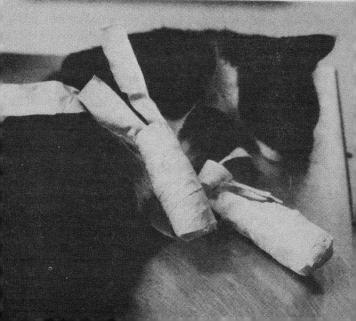

arrival home so as to prevent long-term constipation, loss of appetite, and so forth. If the cat does not begin eating, drinking, urinating, and defecating normally within forty-eight hours, give Vaseline℠ daily—about one tablespoon on the nose—until the situation improves. Do not be misled into believing the cat is inactive because of the declaw. Tend to the anesthesia aftereffects.

As the days pass, the owner must be aware also that there will be some scabbing. Many cats will chew at the scabs; they are what we call "scab pickers." The result will be that the cat will suddenly start limping on one or more feet several days after surgery. Usually, the condition fades as the area reheals. Occasionally, if the cat is the type who picks at the scab constantly, the vet may prescribe an antibiotic to assist healing, just as is done when a cat irritates other parts of the body, refusing to allow them to heal naturally (as if often true of fight wounds, abcesses, spay incisions, ear infections, cuts, and such). If you realize you have a "scab picker," you can distract him by putting *small* dabs of butter here and there on his body. He'll devote his attention, licking and picking, to them rather than the scabs.

The most relevant point for the owner to bear in mind is that declaw is totally external, does not involve body chemistry, and therefore cannot present anything other than a superficial situation. It does not in any way justify all the nonsense ascribed to it.

Along this line, I would suggest you not patronize a vet who tries to make declaw a major issue. In fact, never patronize any doctor who seems reluctant to perform any normal treatment or surgery. Usually people don't like things they aren't good at.

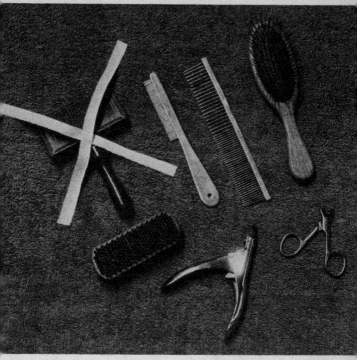

The slicker brush (covered by big X) is not suitable for grooming cats. But other tools shown here are suitable. Those in top row are fine-toothed comb, Greyhound® comb, and pin brush. Bottom row: rubber brush, inexpensive guillotine-type nail clipper, quality nail clipper.

Grooming— "The Cat's Meow"

A well-groomed cat is, you might say, the cat's meow. And anyone living with a cat knows cats like

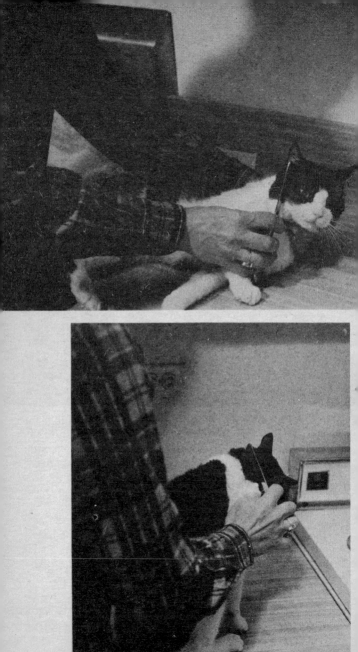

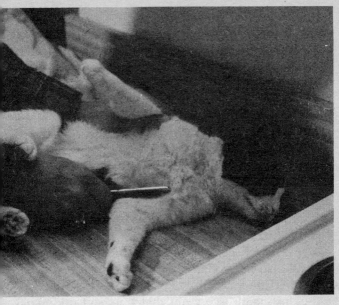

e sure to comb sides of head, back of neck, underarms, nd stomach.

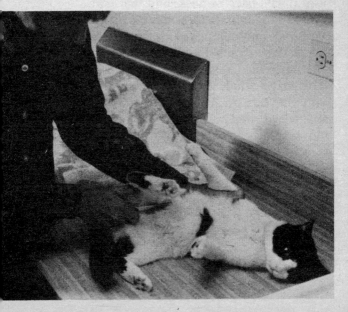

to be well-groomed, beautiful, clean. They do take care of some details themselves; in fact, their attitude generally is that they can take care of everything themselves. But we know better.

The accompanying photograph shows the implements appropriate for grooming our feline friends, even those who become enemies the instant you pick up a comb. (Note: the slicker brush is not to be used on cats. IT HURTS!) Now just go ahead and groom, as follows.

Short-haired cats with little or no undercoat are best groomed with the rubber brush, using the short side of the brush *with* the grain of the coat.

Short-haired cats with a good deal of undercoat should also be groomed with the rubber brush and with the fine-toothed comb as well. This comb has very close teeth to get out that fine, soft undercoat, much of which you will find on either side of the head (face), back of neck, and rear end.

Semi-long-haired cats may be brushed with the pin brush and combed with the fine-toothed comb. If the coat seems too heavy for the fine-toothed comb, use the Greyhound™ comb.

Heavily coated, long-haired cats are best brushed with the pin brush, section by section, and then combed with the Greyhound™ comb. Persians, Angoras, and similar cats should be brushed and combed daily. Otherwise, you will end up having them shaved to get rid of the mats. Regular bathing also helps keep the coat mat-free, provided the cat is mat-free before bathing. Pay particular attention to combing the stomach, sides, throat, sides of head, back of neck, and underarms.

To bathe a cat, first brush and comb thoroughly. Then, if the cat is declawed, put him in the kitchen

To bathe a cat, hold it by the nape of the neck in the sink.

sink or wash basin and proceed. If he has claws, you will generally find him easier to bathe if you lean a screen or a little wooden lattice against the back or side of the sink for him to dig into.

Pour or spray water down over the cat while holding him by the nape of the neck, as the accom-

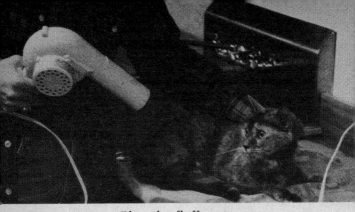

Blow-dry fluffy cats.

panying photograph shows. (Do not expect him to sit or stand in a tub full of water!) Then pour on a well-diluted protein shampoo for animals, which is available from pet shops. (Do not use human products in this regard. They are intended for a different pH and will be harsh on the pet. This advice includes baby shampoo; it's for babies, not pets.) Lather well, rinse off thoroughly. Wrap the cat in a towel and rub dry if short-haired or blot dry if long-haired.

Long-haired cats must not be *rubbed* when wet either to shampoo or rinse since rubbing creates mats. Work shampoo down through the coat with your hands and simply pour rinse or fabric-softener rinse (see de-allergizing instructions in section on page 96) on a very heavily coated cat. Blot with a towel and blow-dry the coat on medium setting *while combing and brushing.* You'll find the cat quickly becomes accustomed to the sensation, finds it pleasant, and lies still to be blown dry.

Most house cats need bathing a couple of times a year; long-hairs obviously need it more often.

While bathing as well as brushing or combing your cat, check him for ticks, fleas, cuts, and tapeworm segments under his tail (they look like little grains of rice). Consult your veterinarian about treatment.

Ear Care

If you have more than one cat, you probably will not have to clean ears, since they will do so for each other. Just check to be sure that is the case by looking inside the ears to see whether there is any dirt or oily buildup.

To clean the ears yourself, use a cotton swab with a little mineral oil or alcohol and work gently. Remove all the dirt and wax.

If you find black crumbly material in the ears, clean it all out and get some ear mite medication from your veterinarian. Use it at least every third day for a minimum of three weeks, removing the dead mites with a swab every time. The eggs are transparent and will not be seen during the three-week period in which they will be hatching. So use the medication for three weeks minimum. If the cat has abscesses around the ears from scratching at the mites, have your veterinarian treat the cat with antibiotics while the abscesses heal and you clean up the mites. You will probably also need to treat the abscesses at home with ointment prescribed by the veterinarian.

Eye Care

In grooming your cat, you may notice a discharge from the eyes if other cats are not cleaning it out. Wipe it out with warm water on a piece of cotton, and then watch to see how much builds up after the eye is clean. If there is enough buildup or discharge to be noticed daily, take your cat to a veterinary ophthalmologist for examination and treatment. He isn't likely to prescribe glasses, but chances are he can provide help in terms of medication that will save Kitty pain and loss of vision. You may be interested to know that often runny eyes result from respiratory viruses—easily treated with vitamin C.

Hairballs

Cats vomit, cough, choke, and become constipated from the hair they ingest when grooming (licking) themselves and each other IF THE OWNER DOES NOT COMB OR BRUSH THE CATS REGULARLY. Each cat should be brushed or combed as often as required by the nature of the coat. It is ridiculous for me to hand out advice to you to use Vaseline™ to help the cat pass the hairballs and soothe the systems when what you really need is a push (swift kick?) in the direction of grooming. Perhaps you will be better motivated if I tell you that using Vaseline™ or other similar products is deleterious to the cat's health because these substances create vitamin deficiencies.

Nail Cutting

If you have cats who are not declawed or you take in a kitten too young to declaw (under twelve weeks) or an older cat whose health does not permit anesthesia or surgery—or if you have cats whose front feet have been declawed but not the rear—those claws must be cut!

Just think about it: if the claws are not cut, the only alternative to their growing around in a circle into the bottom of the cat's feet is for the cat to scratch, bite, or break them off. Obviously, most cats will not be able to wear down the nails on their back feet in any of these ways; nor can they wear down the dewclaws (tiny claws on the inside of the front legs *above* the feet). It is these back claws and dewclaws that we most commonly find grown into the feet or legs, resulting in infected pads with pus oozing from them—and what an odor!

At this stage veterinary work is needed to remove the nail surgically, suture the foot, and bandage it. The cat is given injectable antibiotics and then put on oral medication at home. The bandage is removed after a day or two, and the paw soaked at least three times daily in diluted Betadine™ solution. All of this and the months of pain the cat has already been subjected to are inexcusable results of not cutting nails.

Two types of nail clippers are shown in the photo of grooming tools earlier in this chapter. The guillotine type is commonly available at low cost in most pet stores. The other kind—specially made for cats—is generally available only through veterinary surgical-supply houses, although some high-quality pet shops carry them. These clippers generally cost at least twice what the guillotine type does, but they're well worth it.

The nails should be kept cut back to within about a quarter-inch of the base. If you have not been cutting nails, getting them cut back to there will necessitate cutting through the "quick," the tiny blood supply that grows down nails almost to the tip. Since the quick grows almost to the tip of the

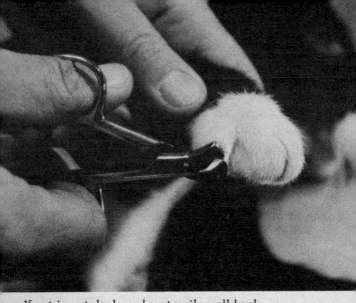

If cat is not declawed, cut nails well back.

Dewclaws on inside of front and rear legs require particular attention.

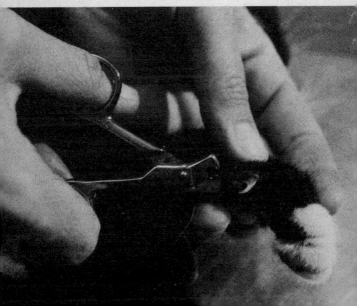

nail, however long the nail grows, and recedes if the nails are cut or worn back constantly, you must cut through it only once if thereafter you will cut the nails back to the quick every week.

When you cut through the quick, the nail will of course bleed. How much and for how long depend upon how long the nail and wide the quick have grown. No cat bleeds to death through his nails, but he surely can make a mess around your house. He won't feel the bleeding and will keep walking around. Be prepared to confine him in a small bathroom, crate, or cat carrier lined with newspapers for several hours. I do not recommend the many products sold to stop such bleeding because most of them sting considerably and are effective only when there is minimal bleeding since the flow of blood washes off the styptic material.

If the nails have been permitted to grow uncut for a period of years, expect them to bleed for some hours, or to start bleeding again a few days later when the cat scratches something hard. This bleeding is natural and harmless to the cat, but you should keep him in an appropriate room until he's beyond this point.

Once the nails are cut back and thereafter clipped back to the quick *every week*, you of course won't have to be bothered with the bleeding again.

I also caution you not to forget the dewclaws even though they don't scratch you or the furniture. And check to see whether your cat has rear dewclaws. Some do. If your cat is polydactyl (has extra toes), check *between* the obvious toes to see whether there are also miniature toes there that have claws. It is particularly important that the nails on polydactyl cats be cut well back frequently. Lack of space for those extra toes allows no excess room for the growth of nails. Big Foot won't look so macho in bandages.

How to De-allergize a Cat

Allergic to your cat? Join a few million others. And be happy to learn there's an easy, inexpensive solution that works to solve the problem!

Before I explain it, let's talk about what you're allergic to—dander, what in human terms is called dandruff.

All of us shed dead skin in some way; if we didn't, we wouldn't be alive. Excessive dander, though, is not normal. So first you must be sure the cat's skin is kept in proper condition to avoid unnecessary dryness and shedding. Fat cats have poor skin and shed excessively; cats eating canned food and soft-moist food shed excessively. The answer to both situations is clear and in your hands (see the section on diet, page 51).

Beyond that, at a pet shop buy a coat conditioner that can be added to the cat's food. The least expensive, most effective, and most widely available I know of is an oil called Linatone™. Use this additive every day for a minimum of three months and during the winter if your home is warm and dry.

Now consider the fact that most people are more allergic to cats than to dogs. Do you know why? Because most people don't groom or bathe cats, who consequently walk around with a life-time buildup of dander. Long-haired cats should be combed regularly and gently with a fine-toothed metal comb. Short-haired cats should be brushed with a rubber brush and combed with a very fine-toothed metal comb. Cats love to be groomed if you do so regularly! They may be bathed in a sink, as explained on page 88.

Besides de-allergizing your pet, you must also clean up the dander that is all over your house. Vacuum thoroughly. Wipe all counters and furniture. Wash bedspreads, sheets, throw rugs, slip covers, and the like. It may take several housecleanings to de-allergize your home, so keep at it. Otherwise, you and your pet will simply be picking up loose dander from the house even after the pet himself has been de-allergized.

Now let me tell you how to de-allergize your cat. Comb and brush his coat well. Bathe him in a good quality, watered-down, tearless protein shampoo *for pets* available in any pet shop. Bathe the cat (see page 89) twice, and rinse out the shampoo *very well*. Next towel off excess water while the cat is in the tub. Then pour over him, saturating the coat totally, a solution of one part fabric softener—preferably Downy—and four parts water. Work it into the coat and *don't rinse it off.* Just dry your pet with a towel or hair dryer, whatever you would normally use. This solution coats the hair and skin and keeps the dander down quite effectively.

De-allergize your cat every six weeks or so. You may find you can wait eight or ten weeks, or that you need to do it every four weeks. Expect to do it more often at the beginning because there will still be dander around the house that the cat will pick up in his coat. And keep cleaning the house extra-thoroughly at the beginning to get up that long-accumulated dander that is everywhere. You will of course end up with a de-allergized house, too!

Hot-Weather Care

Fortunately, cats can tolerate high temperatures better than humans or dogs. So any place you can live will do for your cat as well. Generally, cats prefer higher temperatures than we do, lying in the sun on the hottest of days. So don't bother leaving the air conditioner on for your felines.

If you must transport your cat during extremely hot weather, make up a small ice pack to go in the carrier. You can freeze a block of ice inside a plastic bag or get a couple of cold packs made for use on camping trips. Sporting-goods stores generally have them. You just put them in the freezer for a few hours and then pack them in the carrier with the cat. They are quite effective and will last an entire day or longer. Obviously, no pet should be left shut in a closed car in the sun or even in the shade in very hot weather—cold pack or no. Opening a car window a bit helps—but very little. A cat in a carrier in a hot car is only too likely to suffocate. And if you let the cat out of the carrier, you can't open the window given that cats can squeeze through the tiniest openings. So take the cat—in his carrier— along with you. He can sit at your feet in safety for hours.

Cold-Weather Care

Obviously, your cat can live in your house at whatever temperature you can. All of us cat people notice, however, that our cats can always find the softest, warmest place, and so we realize they truly love warmth.

Providing warm radiators at today's fuel costs is problematical to say the least. An easy, inexpensive way to maintain Kitty's favorite bit of Florida in a cold New England winter is with a heat lamp. Do note that the bulb must be placed in a porcelain socket and should be suspended about four to six feet away from Kitty's nest. I have six such lamps in my home, generally turned on sixteen hours a day from mid-October to mid-April. All the cats love them!

If you have occasion to travel with your cat during cold weather, simply put a good heavy towel in the carrier. If the weather is excessively cold (well below freezing) and you will be outdoors for a lengthy period, put a hot-water bottle in the carrier before leaving home. But don't worry. That little carrier will stay very warm inside just from Kitty's body heat.

Windows, Balconies, and Space in General

A sight that I will never become inured to is that of a cat owner arriving at the clinic's door with a badly injured, often dying or dead cat in arms, thinking we offer emergency service or miracles. They always say: "He sat on that window sill for years, and for some reason today he fell off—eleven stories."

Cat owners must realize that cats do not have the depth perception of humans, nor do they have the power to figure out the relationship of objects in

space. They walk off windowsills, balconies, fire escapes, and so forth, not having the faintest idea what lies ahead, or better said, what doesn't lie ahead.

With the onset of warm weather each year, millions of cat owners open windows that have been closed all winter and shortly thereafter cats (and dogs) fall through space. This phenomenon even has a name: high-rise syndrome. It is a terrible, stupid tragedy.

Windows should have screens well fastened into them so that cats cannot push them out. Or the windows should be opened only a couple of inches *at the top*. Casement windows require special screens. Terraces and balconies must be enclosed.

OR DON'T HAVE CATS!

Traveling with a Cat

Traveling with a cat is the alternative to leaving him home or boarding. Leaving the cat home is preferable if you can get a friend to come in to feed and change litter. A cat can stay alone up to five days without anyone coming in if you leave two big bowls of water, two clean litter trays, and exactly five days' food (dry, of course). If he eats it all in two days, don't worry; he won't starve.

If you must travel with your cat, go to your veterinarian and have your cat get all inoculations and a checkup right before leaving. Get a travel health certificate in case you need it.

For prolonged hours in a car, your cat should have a crate, as described on page 111, with a litter box and water. Do *not* leave food in the crate. The cat should be in the crate at all times in the car for both his safety and yours. When you arrive wherever you will be staying, carry the crate containing the cat, litter, and water into your room, *close the door*, and only then open the door of the crate. The cat will leave the crate or not, as he pleases. He will in any event be able to find his litter and water. Before

you leave a motel room, put the cat back into the
crate and lock it so that an unsuspecting chamber-
maid doesn't lose your cat out an open door or
window.

Feed a traveling cat the usual meal once a day in
the morning, but feed him a good deal less than
usual. Since the cat is inactive, he needs less food. If
you feed the normal amount and the cat eats it, he
will be uncomfortable in the crate. So it is much
kinder to feed less. Obviously, you should travel
with a supply of the cat's accustomed food, litter,
and a small amount of water for emergencies. You
should also have with you a small container of
Vaseline® in case the cat becomes constipated from
inactivity (put a large dab on the nose to be licked
off) and some kaopectate (get prior instructions from
your vet) in case of diarrhea occasioned by change
of environment or water.

Before leaving home, be sure the cat is wearing a
collar with some form of identification in case of an
accident. Have your name, address, and phone number and someone else's phone number on the tag.

Motels are generally not a problem for cat owners
since the management rarely realizes you have a
cat. Most of the major chains accept pets anyway. I
assume you have a declawed cat or one with well-
cut nails so no damage will be done to result in
future restrictions imposed on the rest of us.

Boarding Cats

Preferably cats remain at home when their owners
leave town. The ideal is to have a cat person come

in daily, feed, medicate, change litter, clean water dishes, groom as necessary, and generally care for your cats.

If you board them in a kennel facility (one with cages), make sure each cat is required to have been vaccinated within the past year (I prefer six months) and to have been checked for feline leukemia. Also make sure each cat is gone over carefully when it arrives to keep out any that have fleas, ticks, respiratory diseases, and other obvious disorders.

If the cats are boarded in someone's home, all cats should have been vaccinated, checked for feline leukemia, neutered, and declawed. The neutering and declawing are extremely important in preventing your cats from being subjected to possible aggression from unneutered or undeclawed cats.

Whatever the arrangement, make sure cleanliness, kindness, and care and knowledge of cats prevails. In other words, the local dog kennel that will take your cat as a favor is not a good idea.

3

THE TRIMMINGS

Toys

All cats like expensive, special-order, designer toys such as:

- Plastic spoons
- Spools (sans thread)
- Egg-shaped plastic containers such as those used for packaging panty hose
- Strings, yarn, rubber bands—all to be *avoided* since cats swallow them and they are lethal if caught in the stomach or intestines
- Cotton swabs
- Feathers
- Small balls—rubber, aluminum foil (not to be eaten), wads of paper
- Thin wooden dowels, three to four inches long—better than pens and pencils
- Corks
- Cardboard tubes from toilet paper
- Catnip—"pot" for cats (my cats are zany enough without it)
- Other cats' tails or their own on occasion
- Boxes and paper bags
- Anything else that isn't glued down, including almost everything of great value to you

Litter Pans

INVENTORS, PLEASE READ THIS!

The world needs a high-sided, non-stick-to-it-surface, *weighted* litter pan with no rim on which cat can rest feet. You see, the litter pans with high sides are really dishpans of soft plastic to which everything solid adheres. The lower-sided litter pans are made of hard, smooth plastic to which nothing sticks, but everything falls over the side. All of the pans are light enough to be tipped over by a cat who puts feet on edges of the pan while using it. And my cats don't like small covered litter boxes because one cat can easily corner another inside it—which is bound to happen with many cats living together.

My solution: litter tray (dishpan type) in a wooden crate, attached to the crate at one end with a snap and shock cord so that it cannot be turned over; I put other litter trays in a stall shower. It is not really necessary to have three or four litter trays for, say, fourteen cats, but on days when I don't get home for twelve or fourteen hours, the cats have a little more "toilet" space. Not entirely satisfactory, but passable until a genius reads the foregoing and designs the ideal litter pan.

You will undoubtedly find means of your own. At any rate, put under the tray a towel on which litter can be wiped from feet (rather than tracked), unless you have a cat like Sarah, who pees on the towel. Ah, I do have one of each (problem, that is).

To reinforce what I say on page 116, let me strongly recommend that you use a clay litter (cats don't like the green stuff, and the wood-shavings type makes a dreadful mess), finely ground so as not to track easily, preferably with no "deodorizer" added to dissuade the cats. (I use Poise or Attasan litter, which you can buy from feed dealers.) Put it in the box only enough to cover the bottom lightly, usually two or three cups. Change it frequently; cats hate dirty litter!

Warning: Clean the litter pans with hot water, not "cleaning" products, many of which contain substances toxic to cats. Hot water will do the job more than adequately, and at much lower cost. Also, avoid deodorizing and/or antiseptic sprays. They may be as harmful to cats as the cleaning products.

Carriers

Every cat should have a carrier to go to the veterinarian's office, to move to a new house, to go to the groomer (if you can't manage).

DO NOT TRY TO TAKE YOUR CAT OUT OF THE HOUSE ON YOUR SHOULDER, IN YOUR FAVORITE TOTE BAG, OR ON A LEASH. CATS MUST BE TRANSPORTED IN ESCAPE-PROOF CARRIERS. Nothing else will do.

Most cat owners get mentally involved in carrier features such as ventilation and view—everything but "escape-proof." Which is the *important* aspect. In buying a carrier, make sure the fasteners are secure and firmly affixed to the box. Carriers that open at the end are hard to get cats into and out of. Top-openers are preferable, side-openers next in line.

The carrier should just barely accommodate the

Thomas tries out one of our favorite top-opening carriers.

End-opening carriers are often difficult to use with hard-to-handle cats.

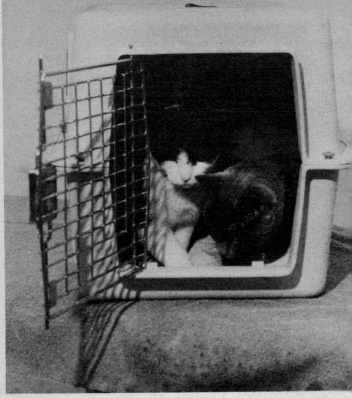

Fiberglass crate, Vari-Kennel #100p, is ideal for carrying two cats, as Thomas and Meg demonstrate.

cat or cats. Excess space lets them slide around, a very insecure feeling for the cats.

Although I have heard all kinds of stories about cats liking uncovered carriers or covered carriers, so as to see out or not see out, I have no reason to think either is important to the cat. Of the fifty to one hundred cats at a time that I see in carriers, none has expressed any desire to see or not to see— sleep being the greatest interest.

Ventilation holes, however, are indeed significant, but they must be such that the cat cannot tear or chew them into escape routes.

Put lots of shredded newspaper into the bottom of the carrier so that the cat is not distraught if he must urinate, defecate, or vomit while in the carrier. Toys, by contrast, simply take up space and serve no purpose. A piece of your favorite, well-worn underwear likewise serves no purpose. He won't forget you anyway.

In an emergency, if you have no carrier, you can alays put a cat in a pillow case or cloth laundry

Vari-Kennel (Sky Kennel) #200p accommodates one cat, litter box, and dishes.

A cat may be carried quite easily in a tied pillow case.

bag and tie a knot in the top. This makes an excellent escape-proof bag that will not stress the cat. Carry it like a sack, by the top, no support underneath. You know how much cats love to curl up inside things! And yes, he can breathe through the porous cloth.

If you have difficulty getting hold of your cat to put him in anything, you might try scooping him up with a pillow case. Just put the opening over the cat and lift him up quickly into the pillow case. Then either tie the pillow case or put it and the cat inside a carrier. Don't worry about how the cat will get out of the case inside the carrier. Just leave the case untied; the cat will manage the rest.

Crates for Cats

At some time in the life of every cat there will be a reason to confine the cat tightly. It may be in order to make sure he urinates; to make sure there is no blood in the urine; to get a fecal sample to check for parasites; to see which cat is having physical problems of one sort or another; to prevent the cat's getting into fresh paint or some poisonous substance, and so forth. So it is imperative that anyone with more than two cats have a good crate to confine a cat in. (If you have only two cats, you can confine one in the bathroom, one out.)

Several types are available. I personally prefer the fiberglass type since litter will remain in the crate. Also, I find cats more content in the enclosed crates; few even try to escape. And since the cat may well be spending several days or even weeks in the crate, it may as well be comfortable and you free of guilt feelings.

Also buy a litter container that fits into the crate easily, leaving the maximum amount of space for the cat to lie down comfortably. The crate should have space for water and food dishes of limited proportion.

It's not a bad idea to leave the crate sitting around open so the cats can get used to it. I would also emphasize, however, that it should never be used for punishment. In other words, don't put the cat in the crate every time you get mad at him. The crate will then become a very negative place, totally unsatisfactory for confinement of a sick cat.

Collars, Harnesses, Leashes

At other points in this book I suggest that a collar might be necessary to control a cat in certain circumstances. Even a leash attached to the collar to give you a little leverage!

But aside from that, why would you want your cat to have a collar, leash, or harness?

If you think your cat needs a collar for discipline, get a tiny leather or plastic one and a leash of the same weight.

Otherwise, you won't need to buy collar or leash. Given the disease situation in the outside world, you certainly won't be teaching your cat to walk on a leash out there. If he must leave the safety of the house, he will be secure in his carrier, away from other cats and dogs and unable to escape and get hurt.

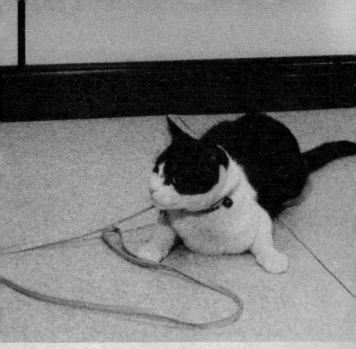

Thomas clearly resents leash and collar because he's now so well behaved he doesn't need them. But he's so photogenic he seemed like the perfect model.

Beds for Cats

You'll probably wonder why your cat should have a bed since he sleeps on yours. Then he shouldn't.

But many cats do need beds for one reason or another—lack of soft furniture for them, or lack of enough soft furniture if you have many cats. Many cats, lacking a bed, sleep in their litter boxes. There is no harm except that they often spill litter and also expose themselves to an extraordinary amount of litter dust, which in turn may create some respira-

Bookcases built into walls next to author's bed become beds for Matilda, Ivy, and Marshmallow.

tory problems. Cats will particularly sleep in litter boxes containing shredded paper. They're comfortable!

You'll see many cute, comfortable cat beds on the market. Remember, cats like *little* places, so don't buy a big luxurious bed. Think small. I have had shelves built into the wall on either side of my bed and put pillows in them. Many of the cats sleep there, sort of like bunk beds.

Important: cover each bed or pillow with a pillow

case or towel that can be washed. Wash them frequently and you will find very little cat hair around
the house, since most of it, naturally, is deposited
where the cats sleep.

The great disadvantage to cat trees and houses
permanently covered with carpeting is that it can
only be vacuumed, not removed and washed several times a week.

So think ahead when setting up cat beds; think
"wash it!"

Old cardboard boxes provide endless play places.

4

BEHAVIOR

Housebreaking a Cat

Housebreaking a cat? Why, everyone knows all cats use litter automatically. Or so "they" say. But judging from the number of calls and letters I get about cats using the bed, the rug, the chair instead of their litter trays, plenty of cats must have housebreaking problems of one kind or another. Fortunately, many of these problems are solved by correcting mechanical errors on the part of the owner.

First, what kind of litter are you using? Cats generally prefer the clay litter and are averse to using the green stuff and other material like wood shavings. So begin by buying a good white clay litter. Try to buy a brand available in twenty-five- or fifty-pound bags so you will not hesitate to change litter often. Also, get the cleanest, most dust-free, most finely ground litter available in your area. Big chunks of clay are readily tracked all over the house. Usually, you do best with the litters sold by professional feed dealers (listed in the Yellow Pages). You want a dust-free litter because many cats use litter frequently or lie in it. If there is a good deal of dust, they begin to show signs of respiratory distress such as wheezing and coughing. Of course, *you* will appreciate the lower dust content too because you won't see that cloud of dust settling on your furniture every time Kitty emerges from the litter box.

Second, now that you have the right type of litter, put the right amount in the box. You should use just enough to cover the bottom lightly (usually between two and three cups)—and try changing it often. I change three litter boxes two or three times a day for twelve cats. Felines *hate* dirty litter and generally won't use it. You actually could be forcing your cat away from the litter box.

Third, where to put the box? In a place of easy access. My litter boxes are inside a large crate (which is on a shelf about two and a half feet off the floor to prevent the dogs from getting in the litter) and in the stall shower. Putting the box inside a crate or stall shower prevents the litter from being kicked all over the room and conceals it from the eyes of those friends not enamored of what is usually found in cat litter. For your own convenience, learn to put a paper mat under the litter tray in the crate. The paper can soak up any urine that runs over the side of the tray if the cat urinates against the corner or with its legs up on the side of the tray. Cat urine smelling as it does, you'll find life a bit pleasanter if there's a mat under the tray that can be thrown away quickly when it smells. Place an old turkish towel at the entrance to the crate or under the tray if it is not in a crate so that the cat wipes his feet on the towel when leaving the tray. In this way litter is less apt to be tracked all over the house.

Of course, the ideal spot for the litter box is the bathtub or stall shower if it's convenient for you. Wherever you put the litter, though, be sure there is never a closed door between the cat and the litter.

So you've changed the litter, put the box in an accessible place, and now want to know what to do to get Kitty to use it. Whenever you're out of the house, confine Kitty in the room with the litter and water. If possible, use a *small* room like a bathroom. Kitty will not want to use the floor and then have to sit in the room with the results. Rather, he will prefer to use the box so he can cover his leavings with litter and spend the rest of the day pleasantly. So confinement will deal with the problem when you are not home. If perchance a "small room" is not small enough to be effective, confine Kitty in a crate with a litter tray and litter. This will litter-train a non-litter-user.

When you're home, Kitty may have the run of the house *under your watchful eye.* If you're too busy to be watchful, then confine Kitty with litter. When you sleep at night, also confine Kitty with the litter. You may put a bed in his room if it makes you feel any better. If he urinates or defecates in the bed, however, remove it.

You will find the housebreaking pattern easier to deal with if you feed your cat once a day in the morning. (See diet section, page 51; do not overfeed!) Then Kitty's body will be in the habit of urinating and defecating in the morning. You can change the litter then, and Kitty will have clean litter until the next morning. He may use the litter to urinate again during the day, but rarely do normal, properly fed, worm-free cats defecate more than once a day. And many urinate only once a day.

If you have more than one cat, confine all cats with the litter, but provide more than one litter tray.

Often the dominance pattern among cats is such that one cat's very presence intimidates another from using the litter. I have a cat who used to sit outside the litter, waiting to attack the others as they used it. With a little greater dominance on my part, however, he has learned that I won't permit him to threaten the others, and they now use the litter with impunity. This pattern is very common; don't overlook it if you have more than one cat.

Along with your confining the cat and keeping him under your eye, you will have to consider the places in the house that have become his favorites. Treat them with a neutralizer to kill the smell of urine (there are products made to neutralize dog urine odors which work well for cat urine also, particularly Dog-Tex®). Cover these spots with furniture and boxes so as to make them inaccessible. You must break the habit, as well as create a new pattern.

If your cat tends only to urinate out of the box, consider the possibility of chronic urinary tract problems. For the sake of future prevention and better housebreaking, give your cat 500 mg. of vitamin C twice a day, either liquid or tablet, both available at health food or drugstores. Vitamin C is an excellent acidifier and may well serve as a long-term preventive as well as effective current treatment. It is easy to correct housebreaking problems with a well cat, but almost impossible with a sick one.

If your cat only defecates outside the box or both urinates and defecates outside the box, follow all the foregoing advice on housebreaking and also consider whether you have been overfeeding. Cut food by two-thirds and see what happens!

If you are litter-training a kitten, simply make sure the litter is within reach of the tiny one. Kittens have no more problems than adults. In fact, probably fewer, but they must be able to reach the litter quickly.

It may seem strange, but I find that street cats have few housebreaking difficulties. Finely bred cats, on the other hand, seem frequently to have such problems. Since we also find that finely bred, highly domesticated dogs do not housebreak themselves as readily as, say, the basic farm dog, I infer that breeding for looks has resulted in a loss of instinctive behavior. This is not to suggest, however, that finely bred cats with housebreaking problems are "incurable." Far from it. You simply must make things work by doing everything right—like changing the litter frequently, using good clay litter, providing sufficient litter boxes if more than one cat is involved, confining the cat with the litter when you are out, feeding properly, and so forth. If you derive extra pleasure from your long-haired beauty, a little more effort on the litter training is a small price to pay.

Territorial Urinating

If you have several dominant, albeit neutered, toms, you may have a "territorial spraying" problem. That is, they work out their ego conflicts by urinating around the house, covering each other's scent as a dominance mechanism. Some may of course actually have urinary tract infections too. In any case, this behavior ceases if all cats receive Mega C Plus powder (see page 25) or ascorbic acid crystals in their food or a 500-mg. tablet of vitamin C twice a day. Undoubtedly, it corrects urinary tract infec-

tions where they occur, but I also theorize that vitamin C makes all their urine smell the same to them
and therefore eliminates the need for one cat to
cover another's scent. Can't prove it—but it works!

The Feline Beaver—
Chewing Plants, Furniture,
Wool, Shoes . . .

At first you blamed the dog for the chewed shoes;
but the next time it happened, he was over at your
mother's house playing watchdog while Dad was on
a business trip. That left the cat or the maid. . . .

Cats chew. Or some do at any rate.

Many cats chew plants. Unfortunately, a large
number of household plants are poisonous to dogs and
cats both. Make sure your plants are not poisonous;
call your poison control unit (see your telephone
directory). Remove all dangerous plants from the
house, or at least hang them from the ceiling. (You'll
still have to worry about falling leaves, however, if
the plants are hanging.) Then remove all plants from
the room in which you leave your cats when you're
out. There is no way to keep them from chewing the
plants or the fallen leaves when you're not there to
watch them.

When you're home, discourage the chewing of
plants by watching for the cat to become interested
in them and warning him off with a loud command
before he gets to the plants. Make it very clear that
you will get there as fast as the cat if he threatens
the plants.

Cats who chew wood, leather, and paper usually

do so because of poor diet. (An exception is my eight-year-old pastel tortoiseshell Marta who has found the best way to get lively attention is to chew a manuscript as I work on it. I have offered her to the government as a paper-shredder, but no takers. . . .) Be sure the offending cat is eating DRY cat food, dry. Check for worms and other internal parasites by taking a fecal sample to the veterinarian.

Beware the supposed panacea of feeding the cat one thing or another to stop chewing. Many things will indeed eliminate a chewing syndrome by virtue of leaving the cat satiated to such a degree that he desires to chew nothing except the most tempting of foods. But then you get into the fat cat or chewer dilemma.

Instead, feed properly, check for worms, confine the cat in a safe room or crate when you're out, reminding yourself that as inconvenient as the chewing is for you, it may be even worse for the cat since he may chew poisonous substances or eat splinters of wood that will puncture his intestines. Occasionally it is necessary to feed a cat two or three *small* meals of dry cat food over a day to relieve the pattern of chewing furniture. If necessary, do it. And don't blame the dog.

If you have a cat who chews holes in wool or some other specific fabric (it usually is just one particular fabric, most often wool), you will generally find that the cat is trying to nurse—yes, even at nine years of age—and is sucking on the fabric, sucking holes in it. Since this is instinctive behavior, perhaps attributable to being weaned too young, it is not possible to change the source of it. But since the behavior is usually directed at one fabric, it is possible to avoid leaving that fabric around or to leave the cat in another room. Watch out for those wool blankets and sweaters!

Aggression

Cats bite? Everyone knows dogs bite and cats claw! So how come the two most common problems readers of my magazine column write in about are housebreaking and BITING? Cats do claw, and they also bite. In actuality, some cats claw and bite, some claw only, and others bite only. It all depends upon their nature, their dominance level, and the owner's dominance level. Clawing is less dominant and, if things go unchecked, escalates to biting.

Basically, your cat demands of you that you be the pack leader, top cat, or whatever you wish to call the role. All cats, no matter how soft and submissive, require some degree of dominance on the part of the two-legged one. However, the more dominant the cat, the more dominant the owner must be. Kitty will do everything in his power to force you to the level of control and authority that his own nature requires. And remember, it is not possible to change his nature, as imprinted at birth. So you must simply respond to the situation as it evolves. If you have a cat who is not spayed or castrated, have him or her neutered immediately for the sake of health as well as to curb aggression. Most females calm down within two weeks and get much easier to live with as long as they are kept healthy, thin, and dependent. Males remain males for some weeks and the changes are not as drastic as with a female.

Have the aggressive cat declawed, all four feet. Even if the cat is primarily a biter, declaw is necessary so that you can handle him without fear or damage to yourself. (Also, declaw together with neutering stops aggression among cats fast! Just declaw all cats, all four feet, and neuter them.) Once Kitty is declawed, you begin to assume the leadership role by:

• Being more vocal—in a very severe, authoritative tone—in correcting Kitty *before* he misbehaves, praising good behavior, showing affection when behavior is good. Do *not* under any circumstances try to cajole Kitty. It will not work, and you will reverse roles again. Just use your voice to make your views and demands *very clear*. Believe me, Kitty understands!

• Grab Kitty by the back of the neck when a little "physical guidance" is called for. That is, when he is about to misbehave, grab him by the scruff of the neck, shake him while yelling at him, and toss him away from you. If you are effective, he will appear to be in shock! And you probably won't have to face that particular issue more than a couple more times. A young kitten who bites while playing or teething may seem to you to present special problems because his behavior doesn't seem to fall into the category of "aggression." Actually, it is the precursor to aggression and should be discouraged. Don't permit the kitten to chew on you ("love bites" as people call them); dive-bomb your feet, teeth first; and so forth. Correct the situation as soon as you notice it. Find alternative forms of "play" now, or regret later.

• Putting a collar on Kitty and, if necessary, a leash with which to get hold of him if you are not too adept at the scruff-of-the-neck business. A collar will not be as effective as your hand on the neck, but it will do, especially as you get more adept.

• Reminding yourself frequently throughout this period: "I am the human; he is the cat. I am the human; he is the cat"—until both of you believe it! Getting tough and staying tough is the key. Since you have been a marshmallow (he wouldn't bite if you weren't), you will need to push yourself as much as Kitty. But once you're there, you will maintain your position because if you slip, Kitty will let you know—painfully!

Terrorism

Dominance and Numbers

Those of us who have *many* cats (over ten, over twenty?) frequently encounter the behavioral conditions engendered by "gangs" within our little feline society, usually "macho groups" of tough, dominant cats who terrorize the others.

Now, it's relatively easy to live with one dominant bully and several softer cats. But it's very hard to live with a gang of hoodlums who band together for the express purpose of threatening others and generally making life miserable. It's just too hard for one human being to stay on top of several such monsters.

But those of us who have many cats generally use more than one room or one floor of the house for our "pastime" anyway, so here's what I have done and the pattern several friends have followed.

I have weeded out the macho group by watching their behavior. They are the cats who pounce on rather than being pounced on. They're the cats who stalk versus those who hold their breath while waiting to see who is the target of the moment. I then transferred the macho cats to another area—at present another floor of the building. All dominant behavior ceased immediately. There seems to be a tacit understanding among them that since they are equals (or so near to it that differences don't count), survival will be achieved on a live-and-let-live basis and none other. They never fight. They share space, food, water, sun, and my presence. There is no territorial spraying or other sign of the dominance level, which is extraordinary.

And on the floor they left, peace reigns, the old lady cats are relaxed and happy, stress has been eliminated, and I get much more sleep.

Cats Who Jump on People

Once upon a time a lovely cat lady adopted out the same gorgeous, purry red cat three times and promptly got him back each time. By the third time, she made great effort to find out exactly what was happening. Seems he had only one bad habit: he jumped onto people's backs while they were in the shower (only then). So he got declawed (all four feet, of course) and lives happily ever after in his fourth home.

Then there was the cutest little multicolored tiger kitten "dumped" in front of a humane society one night while I was visiting. Everyone there thought she was the most affectionate, smartest, as well as cutest kitten they had ever seen. Half an hour after she arrived, however, no one wanted her. You see, she had this habit of jumping from the floor onto one's thigh and zooming up the side of the body to land on the top of the head, where she would rip out the hair, whirling-dervish style. I took her home, had her declawed, and have found her charming ever since.

Most cats will stop dive-bombing people once it becomes impossible, even though they will never realize *why* it is impossible. They are simply smart enough not to waste their time.

Garbage

It's easy to spot the pet owners leaving their homes—they take garbage out *every* time they leave.

Moral: if you are dumb or forgetful enough to leave desirable garbage and cat together, you deserve to have to clean it up.

As for when you're home and Kitty is dive-bombing the trash can, I have only one foolproof idea: put the garbage can where you are working in the kitchen as long as you need it. Then put it behind a closed door—closet door, basement door, whatever. Don't think you can keep Kitty out of it any other way; you're only fooling yourself. Yes, if you're very fortunate, you may get a garbage can with metal clamps on the top edges, which your cat can't open. But then your cat is one in a million and very unimaginative.

The Cats' Place in Your Love Life

"How do I get the cats off the bed when I don't want them there?"

Usually the person asking such a question has already discovered that the cats, if shut out of the bedroom, create more havoc than if left in. I have two cats who can put their paws under a door and shake it so hard the noise is deafening. It sounds as if the whole wall would come down; maybe it would, in fact. I also have two cats who will scratch determinedly in the litter box ad nauseam and, if that doesn't get attention, start hurling litter.

So I'm with you folks who figure it's got to be easier to have them in the bedroom. It is.

Realize that your adult cats will be pests at first. But after being thrown off the bed a couple of times and otherwise ignored, they will go elsewhere. Adult cats love to cuddle on the bed with a quiet or sleeping you but they hate being disturbed by any activity. Note how annoyed they get when you try to turn over. They're not going to hang around long once they get the picture.

Kittens, on the other hand, thrive on activity . . . up to a point. They are extremely active and then collapse in total exhaustion. The trick is to exhaust the kitten *before* you and your lover go to bed. Play with the kitten, throw toys, quick, quick, quick— constant activity. Also, it's a good idea to have some new, distracting toy or old favorite that has "disappeared" for a day or two. You get a lot of mileage out of that one.

Do expect to let the cats sleep on the bed when you go to sleep. Otherwise, they will really take an extreme dislike to the entire situation. And cats being cats, you know how determined they can get when pushed too far.

Cats and Lovers
(Cats vs. Lovers, That Is)

There are cats who *attack* new dates—claws and teeth bared, hissing, hair on end. There are also cats who sit purring in new date's lap and then walk casually across the room and pee on his jacket. Mine have always fit into the latter category, if there were any problems at all.

If yours are the attack type, be sure they are declawed, all four feet, please. Get collars on them so you can get hold of them and fling them across the room while you scream as if the world would end in the next five seconds.

More significantly, keep cats on minimum rations and let your new date feed them a bit. As it is, very few thin, neutered cats are truly unpleasant; they need humans too much.

If yours are the pee-on-the-jacket type, hang the jacket up immediately and everything else as well. Follow the same instructions on feeding.

If, of course, your new friend doesn't "like cats," as they say, either (1) he will change his attitude, (2) you will quit seeing him, (3) you will coexist—cats and people—in misery, or (4) the cats will go live somewhere they are wanted. If you get rid of the cats, you will probably find that you and your new "friend" will split within thirty days, unless of course he finds another battleground of interest within your so-called relationship.

Punishment vs. Correction

People often ask how to punish a cat, and I ask, "why? What did the cat do?" Then inevitably I find out the human set up situations in which the cat was out of control and after the disaster thought the cat should be punished. The key to punishment is *eliminating the need for it* by doing everything right to begin with. If you follow all the instructions in this book, you will have no need to punish the cat because you will have prevented the undesirable behavior before it happened.

The substitute for punishment becomes correction beforehand. When you see Kitty eyeing a plant, yell at him not to touch it and move toward him threateningly. That should suffice. When you see him eyeing the table you are setting, yell at him and again move toward him fast before he gets there. Be very stern and authoritative. The threat in your voice should be so severe that Kitty doesn't want to find out anything further about the potentials of the encounter.

And what do you do when punishment is called for because you didn't act fast enough and so must make a point with Kitty? Take him by the back of the neck and shake him fiercely. If you can't handle him that way, get him a collar and grab the collar and shake him. If he eludes you even that way, put a leash on the collar; you can always grab it or step on it as he flies by. Use collar and leash as long as it takes you to get things under control.

You want to approximate as much as possible the manner in which a mother cat disciplines her kittens by taking them by the back of the neck with her teeth and shaking them. As far as Kitty is concerned, you have assumed her role and are expected to act accordingly, whether you want to or not!

New Baby

If you've heard as many crazy, stupid stories about cats and babies as I have, you will know that I am trying to maintain an attitude of calm and control in starting this section. Actually, all of us who love and know cats feel like screaming: "Who told you that? That's stupid! That's crazy! Cats and kids love one another. Cats do not smother babies! Cats do not attack children!" On the other side, "Children do not prefer dogs. Children do not have to torture cats." And so forth, ad nauseam.

If you have a cat and now look at the prospect of bringing a new baby into the house, you have very little to deal with except to be sure you remember to give the cat some attention so he doesn't feel abandoned. He will probably be attracted to the baby because of the food smells about it and the attention focused on it. Other than that, time will provide adequate opportunity for Kitty to get to know a developing infant who will become his friend.

I strongly recommend that any cat who will be playing with a child should be neutered as early as possible and declawed, all four feet. If this is impossible because the cat cannot take anesthesia, the nails should be cut back to the base every week. Neither the cat nor the child understands about claws or their effects. And it's not fair to expect them to.

Let Baby and cat cuddle up and so forth. You can be sure Kitten will leave when the play gets to be too much. You know you can always count on a cat to take the easy way out!

Just be careful not to let Kitty eat Baby's food, or you will end up with a fat cat and a thin child.

Death of a Loved One

Having written on dogs and the death of a loved one, I realize how lucky the canines are compared with the felines under certain circumstances. Dogs can go places so easily that one can say, "Take your dog for lots of walks; do obedience work. Take him visiting. Take him for a ride." But cats, for their own good, seldom leave the house.

So when Kitty loses his best friend, two-legged or four, you must resort to other means to get him out of his doldrums. One friend went so far as to import a mouse, a real one, which Kitty proceeded to ignore anyway.

If there are any toys that will help, get them. Any games? Play them.

Don't resort to favorite foods unless the cat is

literally starving. Otherwise you will simply have a *fat*, depressed cat.

No matter whether the cat has lost a human or animal friend, he can often be cheered and certainly kept busy by a new feline in the house. Some say a kitten is best: more fun, more activity, more acceptable to an older cat. I personally, in placing cats into such situations, make an effort to suit the new addition to the incumbent's personality. If the survivor is easygoing, cuddly, I pick an easygoing, cuddly cat who is a cat's cat: that is, one who is more interested in cats than people. Remember, you're getting a cat for the cat, not a cat for you. The new addition will become your friend soon enough. But if all his attention is for you right now, you have defeated your purpose. If the resident cat is normally a very active, playful cat, get a player, a nonstop roll-and-tumble cat. If the old guy is very aggressive, tough, be sure to get a tough cat who is still a *cat's cat*.

I hope you are fortunate enough to know the local "cat lady," who can supply the right personality. If not, do some thinking and looking yourself. Judge personalities, not looks, age, or sex, which are unimportant. Unfortunately, such factors are exactly what most people focus on.

One good point, however: even if you bring a hyperactive live wire in to a sweet, laid-back cat, you *will* keep him busy. It's just not what I had in mind.

Cat in a New House

For some cats, moving to a new house can be the
trauma of a lifetime. For others, it's merely a two-
second shock. I have been extremely intrigued by
the fact that my blind cat is delighted to move, never
gets upset, finds his way around a new house
instantly, and is everybody's favorite guest. Others
of my cats simply don't stir for days, move very
slowly, or bounce around trying to figure out everything at once.

If you have occasion to move, get your cat's new
bathroom set up before introducing Kitty to the new
environment. Carry him in his carrier directly into
the bathroom where the litter is and shut the door,
leaving him there for at least twenty minutes, preferably an hour or more.

While he's sniffing out the new bathroom, make
sure all doors and windows are closed and also any
openings in the new dwelling that he could disappear into. Then open the bathroom door and let him
wander out at his own pace. If the house is enormous,
it might be better to shut off some rooms for a few
days so he can first become accustomed to part of
the place. Cats are so much smaller than we that
they're often overwhelmed by spaces beyond their
comprehension. They become downright scared.

Along the way, of course, introduce Kitty to his
new dining room and to the bedroom he will sleep
in. If he has a favorite pillow or blanket, put it out
for him.

If the house quickly fills with your belongings

and your scent, he will feel comfortable in a hurry. But if the house is full of packed cartons, he will probably pee on them. He's just trying to get a familiar scent around the new house, unpleasant though his action may be to you. So if you can't unpack, leave Kitty in the bathroom until you do. He'll be more relaxed there with his old blanket than wandering around uninhabited rooms dotted with packing cases.

And you won't start off with a peed-upon new home.

New Cat in the House

If you are one of the many who think you just bring a cat or kitten into a house and forget it, forget it! Contrary to common belief, cats do not find litter a mile away (they are cats, not scent hounds), nor do most adjust to new places instantly.

Put your new cat in the room with the litter (and food and water if they are eventually to be kept in that room), and close him there for at least half a day, preferably a full day. Then open the door and allow the cat to find his way out, investigating at his own pace. Do not pick him up and take him on a guided tour. He can only find his way back (to the litter) over ground his feet and nose have already covered. He's not a homing pigeon!

If the food and water are to go in a room other than his bathroom, show them to him once he has adjusted to the rest of the environment. He's not going to die without them in the meantime, and adjusting to the new home is more important than eating. In that regard just follow his inclination and don't be alarmed if he doesn't eat for a few days.

Cat Trapping

You (and I) of course already have sufficient cats, but who could ignore the plight of the homeless strays wandering the edges of residential property, creeping around an urban parking lot or construction site at night? Once in a while, after a long period of regular feeding and talking, you will be able to get to touch a cat who probably was once a house pet. But most often you will not be able to pick up these cats, either to have them neutered and take them in or to find them homes, or even to return them to their outdoor homes in an unbreedable state.

If you are as determined as most of us cat lovers, you will need a live-trap such as the one in the accompanying photograph. Any humane organization, local dog warden, or veterinarian should be able to tell you where to buy or rent a trap. Also, most large sporting-goods stores sell them—unfortunately, for inhumane purposes.

It is relatively easy to trap the majority of cats once you have established a feeding program—that is, feeding them daily in the same place at approximately the same time.

Preparatory to trapping, feed lightly for several days, about half the normal amount for at least two or three days. Do not feed "goodies"; feed routine foods. Then set up your trap or traps at the normal place and time, and place in each one a small portion of *smelly* food like mackerel, tuna, salmon, or chicken liver. Be sure the food is placed well to the back wall of the trap as cats are very expert at reaching the bait without touching the plate that sets off the trap. Once you have set out your traps, just retire a short distance and let the cats investigate and find the food is *inside* the "funny thing." They will then start entering the traps cautiously, relax, and go all the way in to eat. And that's that; the traps will close.

In live-trap, food is placed as deep as possible—well beyond the trip plate.

Trap shown here, demonstrated by a pleased Thomas, is Tomahawk No. 106 from National Live Trap Corp., Route 1, Box 302, Tomahawk, Wis. 54487; phone (715) 453-2249.

If you are trapping several cats using many traps, remove each trapped cat (in his trap) from the scene immediately if possible, setting it at some distance so the others won't see it and become alarmed. Once all your traps are full, take the cats STILL IN THE TRAPS to the veterinarian to be neutered. Don't be concerned about leaving cats in traps twenty-four to forty-eight hours. Just leave them alone. They'll eat and eventually relax. Don't try to transfer them to carriers. Cats who must be trapped cannot be handled and transferred to carriers easily. The veterinarian should receive the cat in the trap and also a carrier to put each cat in after surgery while still lightly anesthetized. Then you may take him home securely and let him out of the carriers under appropriate conditions in the confines of your home or wherever you desire it to be. If you plan to return the cats to the same site, do not return any until all have been trapped. Otherwise you will end up with the same cats again. If the remaining cats have no food source other than what is in the traps, you will obviously get all the cats in a few days. So hold out until you do.

It is important for every cat lover to understand that it is not reasonable or humane to feed homeless cats without having them neutered. If you simply feed them, you will only increase their number and therefore their suffering. We always say that so-called "humaniacs" who feed strays without neutering are playing God and doing a bad job. So let your commitment be to feeding in order to trap and neuter. By the way, don't be surprised at the number of pregnant females. If you trap five females, over five months of age, expect three to be pregnant; and don't be surprised if all five are. They simply get spayed to prevent the birth of the litters as well as to prevent future pregnancies. Pregnant cats are the easiest to trap; they're very hungry all the time.

Your effort is really worthwhile, and the investment in the trap is particularly so because you will be sending considerably less on food in the future (for the cost of feeding four kittens for a month, you could spay their mother and prevent all her future litters), and you will have prevented the birth of more strays destined for the suffering of a homeless life.

Domesticating a Cat

All of us cat folk acquire at one time or another a
wild or simply very frightened cat. Some are the
kind that spook at everything and run. Others are
almost catatonic, often leading some to the conclusion they are retarded, brain-damaged. I have often
heard of and seen such cats so described, but never
has one been so. They all simply had behavioral
problems that some human could tackle and solve
with a little or much effort.

Put the new, fearful cat in a *small* bathroom with
as few unnecessary articles in it as possible. If this
bathroom is generally the one for your other cats,
move their litter outside the door—they'll find it.

For the new cat, put food and water as well as
litter in the small bathroom. *Leave* food and water
available there until the cat is domesticated. The cat
must not leave this room until everything is under
control and the cat is relaxed and handleable.

Because you yourself will use the bathroom for
all its normal purposes, the cat will see you come
and go in a nonthreatening way and will get accustomed to you. Whenever you sense the time is right,
stroke him, talk to him, whatever you can manage.
Remember throughout, however, that eye contact is
threatening, so don't look him in the eye.

My own way of getting a cat positively oriented
in a short period of time is to leave the normal dry
cat food out so the cat may eat when he pleases
(undomesticated cats are too nervous to overeat or
get fat!) but then also once or twice a day to arrive

with less than a teaspoon of some special treat like liver or fish or chicken. The cat is given very little so that he will not become satiated but will want more.

I simply put the goodie on top of the dry cat food in the regular dish and leave. Within a day or two, the cat will be dashing over to me every time I enter

Sparkle and Jasmine both arrived at Pet Clinicare wild, untouchable cats. Now look!

the room. He may not want to be petted or picked up, but he certainly looks forward to my visits. Everything comes along naturally after that.

Once the cat is relaxed, uses the litter, and eats with a minimum of anxiety and skittishness, leave the bathroom door open so that he can wander at will (probably when you're not around). If you have any pets that terrorize him, follow the specific instructions for such a situation (see below and the section on "Terrorism," page 125).

From Pat Windmer's Dog Training Book

Cat Meets Dog*

Once upon a time every farm had cats in the barn and dogs in the pasture and kitchen. Neither the cats nor the dogs nor the farmer ever thought it strange that all lived in harmony, for all were "God's creatures," and that was that.

But as we became an urban nation, our agrarian past receding quickly, we became "cat people" and "dog people." As if there were a difference!

Now, however, with the vast animal population depositing litters and strays at our doors, we are put in contact with all domestic creatures—who don't stop to ask whether it is the door of a "cat person" or a "dog person." And we find we do indeed love them equally—differently perhaps, but equally.

*Reprinted with permission from Pat Widmer's Dog Training Book by Patricia P. Widmer, © 1977. Published by David McKay Company, Inc., and reprinted by New American Library.

This situation can at times present some problems, though. If you're about to get a cat and dog together for the first time, you may be experiencing all kinds of trepidations—and wisely so. They are not likely to kill one another, but the tearing around can get out of hand fast.

Usually a cat, confronted with a new dog, will leap from one safe perch to another, observing the dog, perhaps even approaching it curiously. The dog in turn will probably think this is all a great game and go bounding after the cat. And next thing you know, your previous knicknacks are flying, the cat is hissing and howling and scratching, and the dog is wondering why in the world you're so upset.

To avoid such chaos, put a leash at least six feet long on the dog before introducing the cat. Then, if necessary, you can control the dog and thus the cat also. The cat will not leap about wildly if the dog does not give chase. You will find that if you keep the lid on for a short time, your animals will form a friendship quickly and adjust their play to what you can live with. The worst that can happen is that they'll ignore each other or do an occasional bit of teasing.

Other situations you must be aware of when cat and dog share a house arise from the need to keep cat litter available as well as to feed the cat cat food.

Obviously, if the cat food is reachable, the dog will eat it, leaving none for the cat and upsetting the dog's own diet and housebreaking at the same time. It is therefore necessary to feed the cat in a place that it can jump to readily and safely but which is out of reach of the dog. If your dog is small, the kitchen counter will do. Otherwise, how about the top of the refrigerator or behind a closed door?

Then there's the litter. If there's a dog in the world who doesn't love to eat cat feces from the litter box, we haven't met him. Most dogs would prefer this "delicacy" to anything you can offer. So put the litter—preferably in one of the closed-type litter boxes—up high enough on a table, platform, shelf, or whatever, that the dog can't reach it.

Having solved the logistics of litter and food, all you then need do is stay in command of your happy pack.

Charlie

5

HOW TO ACQUIRE A CAT

I can't imagine anyone who has not already been acquired by a cat, but if you haven't, here goes.

First suggestion: Call your neighborhood "cat lady." You don't know who she is? Ask a veterinarian, pet shop, grooming shop, neighbor who has a cat, grocery-store owner, or the greatest gossip on the block. Find out what felines she (or he) has for adoption. You will probably have to pass a good deal of screening and get an education along with it. There's a better-than-average chance this will result in your getting the right cat with a great deal of veterinary work already done, for which you should reimburse the good lady, plus some. Once you have your cat, take him home, confine him in your bathroom until you can get an appointment for whatever veterinary work remains to be done: inoculations, neutering, feline-leukemia test, declaw, worming, whatever.

Second suggestion: Visit the local humane organizations and select a cat from among the many they shelter. Disease tends to be a problem in many large or poorly run shelters, so try to find an alert, active, friendly cat. And be off to your vet, *at once.*

Third suggestion: Check newspaper ads for cats

for adoption. Many humane individuals—animal workers, as we call them—who care for homeless cats advertise what they have for placement. Again, if you adopt a cat, promptly take him to your vet.

Important: When you call people who advertise, avoid those whose cat had a litter. You may be tempted by the thought of "home-raised kittens." But the fact remains that these are the people who help create the animal overpopulation now resulting in the deaths of so many poor creatures. Most of these thoughtless people, if unable to "get rid of" the kittens easily, will have Mom spayed before it happens again. Just remember, it's up to you. If you take kittens off their hands, you contribute to the problem as well. (We have a policy in the clinic of taking occasional litters for adoption *if the mother comes in for spay at the same time.*) If there is a kitten you particularly want in such a home, at least agree to take it only *after* the mother has been spayed (this can be done when her kittens are five weeks old).

If you want a purebred (specific breed) cat, you should list your requirements with all local shelters, humane organizations, and animal workers. Chances are you will have what you want in a few weeks, I'm sad to say. The world abandons purebreds as readily as mixes.

Patronize a breeder only as a last resort if you cannot find the cat you want elsewhere after at least two months of search. Obviously, buying from a breeder encourages the breeding of more cats. So as a minimum, buy from a breeder (advertising in your local paper or through one of the cat clubs) who breeds few and selectively; also, one who exhibits. In all probability he or she is gaining knowledge and breeding healthier, better-dispositioned cats than one who breeds for dollars alone.

Under no circumstances should you buy from a pet shop or someone who just bred two cats for money or "so they could have kittens." Buying from such sources encourages more breeding of a similar nature—*and more breeding results in more deaths.*

It is of the utmost importance to see that your new cat has prompt veterinary care—a thorough checkup including inoculations, feline-leukemia testing, neutering, worming, and ear mite treatment. And don't think you don't need these precautions just because you get a cat from a friend or "private owner" or "breeder." These steps must be taken unless you get a certificate from a veterinarian attesting that they have already been done. The lack of inoculations and leukemia testing can be lethal. The lack of neutering can lead to the birth of a litter of kittens or a home sprayed top to bottom with cat urine. So don't wait.

6

YOUR PETS AND YOUR DEATH

Most of us who have cats have many. Since they are a minimum of effort even for the aged, we are likely to have many right up to the point of our death. If we are concerned enough to worry about their fate after ours, all kinds of possibilities come to mind.

One of the most popular fantasies I hear is that all the pets should be put to sleep (killed) upon the owner's death because "no one will take care of them, no one will love them, no one can afford them, *they could never be happy with anyone else.*"

This last is the ultimate ego trip and nothing else. Further, I don't believe most departed souls would really wish to cause the destruction of their pets.

So let's proceed to the realistic possibilities.

Retirement Homes

At present there are only a few genuine, top-rate retirement homes for pets throughout the country, but their numbers increase yearly. So you might begin checking around now. Generally, these homes are part of an animal welfare organization. Therefore, it behooves you to investigate the backing organization as well as the retirement home itself.

As far as the quality of the home is concerned, here are the main requirements they should insist on for animals they accept:

- General checkup
- Up-to-date vaccination and recent feline leukemia test
- Neuter or spay
- Declaw (required by the best I have seen) or, alternatively, constant nail cutting (I have never seen this practice followed sufficiently, but certainly could be) to prevent the cats' injuring one another
- Limitations on numbers in given spaces
- Total isolation from shelter and hospital animals
- Easy identification of specific animals

All such homes have contracts and financial demands, of course, and you should investigate these now to see what you can handle and how to go about getting started. While you're at it, ask to see a copy of the contract and be sure it includes visiting rights for whomever you wish to designate.

Relatives and Friends

Only if you have just one or two pets can you hope to have them cared for by friends or relatives. If this course seems like a possibility, try it out by leaving the pets with them for weekends or vacations. *Now* is the time to learn all the pitfalls. Most friends and

relatives will not love your pets as much as they
love you.

Pet Professionals

A "pet professional" or "animal arts professional"
is someone who makes a living in animals: a veterinary technician, a groomer, a trainer, a kennel
operator, a shelter worker, a cat or dog sitter or dog
walker. Most of them make a very poor living and
would consider caring for your pets after your death
if you could leave adequate financial means to provide food, grooming, and veterinary care for the
pets plus something to improve the general life style
of their new guardian; for instance, an amount adequate to cover all monthly costs for your animals
plus a sizable part of the new guardian's rent or
mortgage payment.

It is also my opinion that the monthly maintenance amounts payable to the guardian should cease
upon the death of the last of your pets. Such a
stipulation provides incentive for good care.

Explore all of these alternatives *now*, and begin to
plan for the appropriate one. Please do not believe
they are out of the question because of your limited
means. If you can afford to care for your pets now,
you can afford their future. But you cannot afford to
wait to make your plans.

7

THE CATS ARE DRIVING
ME TO DESPAIR"

SOCIETY'S REFLECTION

When I wrote a book on dog training and care some
few years ago, I was ever mindful of the concept
that the domestic animal—the "pet"—is a divine
gift to show the human's own reflection. And that
reflection is pretty poor in a world full of abandoned,
stray animals starving to death, being hit by cars,
reproducing endlessly, dying of disease. If I did not
feel the need to work with people to improve the
situation, I could very easily become a recluse, unwilling to watch the horrors I cannot turn away
from. As an elderly West Indian woman now living
in Brooklyn told me recently: "The cats are driving
me to despair. Every time I look out, there's another.
I know I have to take them in, have them spayed,
care for them, feed them. But it's endless. The cats
are driving me to despair."

The vast majority of people who pick up this
book could say the same. Very few cat owners have
one cat; very few are ignorant of the strays on the
street. But in case you have any doubt as to how bad
it is, try this: In New York City in 1980, for example,
we are told by City officials and the ASPCA that

there are at least 200,000 stray dogs on the streets of the five boroughs. Figures at Pet Clinicare indicate a minimum of ten times as many cats as dogs, probably twenty to thirty times the number. That means a minimum of 2 million stray cats on the streets in New York City alone. Does this figure speak to you? Does it touch you? Consider too that New York City has one of the lowest per capita animal ownership figures in the country, so almost any other city can boast a *worse* problem.

The only reason cats don't become a major issue with public health authorities generally is the assumption on the part of the public that they control rats and the fact that they do not attack humans or otherwise intrude upon our lives. That's right, a starving cat will run from the people he fears and simply continue starving—to death. A starving dog will intrude upon human property, seeking garbage, and then become hostile if disturbed or threatened. Dogs are *visible*, cats rarely so. I often think the cats' suffering worse because it usually lasts longer. A stray dog will not survive long compared with a cat. In other words, the quick death may be the dog's "advantage." Cats hang on, starving slowly, freezing in winter, losing legs and eyes frequently along the way, becoming almost unrecognizable. Females endure all this suffering plus being bred constantly, often bearing litters three times a year. We who pick them up, trapping where necessary, simply befriending in other cases, know that this suffering must be ended, effectively, quickly, once for all.

To do so, it is necessary to understand first how the cats get on the streets and why they stay there. Most of the reasons are pure ignorance, carelessness, stupidity. We must start by realizing that our domestic cat is not a wild animal able or intended to live outdoors, "living off the land," as the saying goes. We have domesticated these animals and now bear the responsibility for their care. They belong indoors, safe from disease, cars, torture, starvation. CATS SHOULD NEVER GO OUT! (No, they don't dream of going out, fantasize about freedom, and so forth. That's your hangup!)

Yet most do go out. Owners let male cats roam because, if kept indoors, they "spray"; that is, urinate all over furniture, clothes, books, rugs. Of course, if they were castrated, they would not spray, and they'd be much happier, less frustrated.

Owners let females out because they howl when in season, also "spray" urine around the house. Of course, spaying would end the problem easily and make for a healthier, happier cat.

Cats sit in windows—"He likes to watch the people"—and one day fall or walk off. A screen would have prevented this disaster so easily and cheaply.

Owners fail to groom their cats and start sneezing as the house becomes covered with cat hair. The cat is then let out—usually with the hope that he'll get lost or at least spend the majority of his time, and shedding, outdoors. Is two minutes of combing weekly really too much to ask?

Cats are let out because "it's natural." Whatever that means. City cats are permitted to climb the fire escape as if it were a jungle gym especially erected for the cat's pleasure. Of course, it has a top and bottom from which the cat may leave home.

Then there's the owner whose ego requires that he wander around the neighborhood with the cat perched on his shoulder or walking on a leash, until the cat has had enough, is frightened, or whatever, and bolts. Ditto the owner who thinks the cat can go to the vet or groomer without a carrier. The owner who always gets me into a screaming rage is the one who indeed has a carrier but thinks his cat is too special to put into the carrier and insists upon carrying him into the veterinary hospital sans carrier. The unruly German Shepherd inside the door does little for the cat's peace of mind, and one more cat bolts down the street.

And there's the occasional owner who deliberately lets the cat out for "sex" because the cat "needs it." I wonder whether the owner behaves similarly. Probably.

And then there's the most common reason of all for letting a cat out, abandoning a cat, turning a cat in to a shelter, having a cat put to sleep (killed): *SCRATCHING!* Thanks to horror stories about declawing together with high veterinary costs, more cats die from lack of declawing than for any other reason, and our streets are full of cats who could have stayed at home had they not scratched the front of the new speakers or the antique sofa or, worst of all, the new baby.

When you look at these facts, you realize that most strays could have stayed at home given neutering and declawing, and a little information at the same time. After all, most people who neuter and declaw their cats will not be motivated to let them out—nor have need to.

The population on the street now obviously must be reduced by picking up and neutering for adoption all those cats with human orientation. Wild cats probably must be trapped, neutered, and re-

urned to safe areas on occasion, domesticated on
others. (It is absolutely sinful to feed cats on the
street without trapping and neutering them. Fed
cats are that much stronger and able to reproduce
and worsen the situation in a hurry.) But who will
do all that needs to be done?

Obviously, as long as cats are not considered a
health hazard, governmental agencies will not sweep
the streets, picking up cats as they do dogs. And
none of us cat folk would want that. Even among
the non-animal-oriented public, the mass extermina-
tion of any living species that results from "governmental effort" is no longer an acceptable concept.

Humane Organizations: The Solution?

It is equally obvious that the big humane organizations will not solve the problem either. Despite the
oft-heard aphorism that the business of every humane organization is to put itself out of business,
few actually try to do so or even pay lip service to
this grand intent anymore. It can't be because they've
forgotten this purpose; they are constantly reminded
of it by those of us who find their activities inadequate.
So we can only assume it's because a job is a job is a
job (or a paycheck is a paycheck is a paycheck).

But what is the job? The three different points
from which these organizations may be viewed provide three different answers: (1) what they *actually*
do; (2) what the public *thinks* they do; (3) what they
should do.

Let's dispose of some big national organizations

first, since their role requires so few words. They are mainly lobbying organizations. They do not operate shelters, care for animals, deal with the public, or in any way dirty their hands or shoes. They maintain large offices and staffs, tell us they are saving the endangered animals (I hope they are), accredit one another, do "research," and in general spend a helluva lot of tax-exempt contributions.

You are undoubtedly better acquainted with your local humane societies. Their functions *in descending order of budget and numbers* are usually to:

- Receive, shelter briefly, and then kill unwanted pets
- Round up unwanted animals
- Adopt out pets
- Provide veterinary services
- Educate the public
- Spay and neuter animals
- Prosecute cruelty cases

The public generally *thinks* they perform these functions in *this* order:

- Shelter pets
- Prosecute cruelty cases
- Educate the public
- Adopt out pets
- Spay and neuter pets
- Provide veterinary services
- Round up strays
- Kill unwanted animals

So what's wrong that these two lists don't match? Or that *neither* set of priorities will solve the problems of animal overpopulation, suffering, abandonment, cruelty?

No matter how many animals are rounded up and killed by a "humane" organization today, THE STREETS WILL BE FULL AGAIN TOMORROW IF THE PUBLIC HAS NOT DEVELOPED A NEUTERING MENTALITY, has not been educated to stop breeding, start neutering, leashing dogs, keeping cats indoors, treating humanely, feeding properly, training properly, getting adequate vet care, and so forth. This conclusion is clearly demonstrated by the fact that humane organizations and municipal governments have been rounding up and killing excess animals for a hundred years in the United States and the problem is worse, not better.

So the priority must be:

• Provide school and community education programs; make neutering available cheaply; and create an atmosphere of social acceptance for neutering. A survey Pet Clinicare conducted of its clients indicated that 82 percent had not neutered pets previously for financial reasons; 51 percent believed that education—most particularly advertising of low-cost neuter facilities—was primary to end the over-population situation. So the means are as clear as the goal.

• Adopt out animals well. No one should be able to adopt an unneutered pet (Florida now has such a law). No one should be able to buy or adopt a pet without professional counseling on care and warnings against abuse.

• Prosecute abandonments and cruelties actively with the assistance of press coverage and public pressure (no one supports cruelty, but many don't know it exists or the forms it takes).

• Make an effort to trace owners of lost pets, contact them, and find out why the pet was lost. If leash laws were broken, prosecute. If abandonment laws were violated, again prosecute. Return only pets lost for genuine, good reasons.

• By these means eliminate the need for large-scale roundup-shelter-and-kill operations.

What can you do personally? Never give a cent to any organization that adopts out unneutered pets; if your local humane organization claims it does not kill, make sure it does not just ship the animals elsewhere for that purpose; create the social pressure that demands "humane" organizations act as if their own early demise were their goal. Attend meetings, volunteer at a shelter, learn what's happening. You will be appalled to learn that many humane-organization executives spend their time talking dollars and euthanasia methods—not a future that is devoid of homeless animals. (You will also find many of them incredibly well-paid, often uncharitable people.) They walk through their concentration camps for animals as if such facilities were an acceptable concept. Remember, these places are acceptable only as long as the public (YOU!) tolerates the *idea* and puts up the money. By the way, you will notice that all animal-related functions of shelters, humane organizations, and governments are referred to as "animal control." I dream of the day when attitudes change and so do the words—to "animal care."

The shift will take place when the public (YOU!) demands that its contributions and/or taxes be channeled to neutering and education. Then the humane organization employee retirement plans will read "at the cessation of operations of the society" rather than simply "when the employee reaches the age of sixty-five." If such a view seems farfetched, just consider the number of animals who never live to reach retirement age under the current system.

Having recognized the shortcomings of the humane organizations and not holding our breath waiting for them to change, how do we propose an immediate solution to the plight of the animals on the streets? Through the efforts of individual "animal workers" aided by other animal lovers.

To start with, let me give you a little background on some of the animal workers I know.

Your Friendly Neighborhood Cat Lady, a.k.a. "Somebody"

Remember that old sign: "If you're not part of the solution, you may be part of the problem"? Or how about: "To get a job done, ask a busy person"? Or: "Those who can, do; those who can't, write (teach)"? Or try this one: "The next time you see something that makes you think 'Somebody should do something about that,' remember, you're 'somebody'!"

If you have one or two pets, or none, you probably think the neighborhood cat lady or gentleman—who has anywhere from ten to forty cats and dogs, picks up strays, feeds everything on four legs, is frequently seen at midnight with a cat trap—has an uncontrolled love for animals and an uncontrolled absolute lunacy. Actually, most of these people are the "somebodies"—the people who see a job that needs doing and *do* it. They are often what your shrink calls the "compulsives" who simply cannot

A wild cat waits at his feeding station for his "friendly neighborhood cat lady."

without great effort walk away from the obvious need.

No, their eyesight isn't really any sharper than yours when they see that scared little pup or kitten abandoned in a sack in a pitch-black garbage can. They just function at a higher level of awareness for such things, partly because they don't intend to pass it by or even have to stop and think, "Shall I or shan't I?"

They long ago faced up to the fact that there are hundreds of millions of stray animals in the United States at any given moment who need to be fed, housed, neutered, befriended. They have got beyond the point of "What would I do with a stray cat—me of all people?" to the point of "What would the cat do if I didn't pick him up?"

As head of a low-cost spay/neuter clinic in New York City and a "cat lady" myself, I have come to know the others of my ilk intimately and for the most part respectfully. I have also come to understand the frustrations they live with and the total misconception of them by the world around them. In over ten years of TV, radio, and press interviews, I've met only one interviewer—a very philosophically astute young writer for the "Today" program—who ever realized that my animal work arises not from a love of animals but rather from an ability to respond to a need and deal with it effectively, be it a stray dog or a dirty, treeless block (it's now clean and planted). But just to show you where most of the world stands, I must point out that the very cogent interview he wrote was totally scrapped by the chic TV personality who actually interviewed me before the cameras in favor of an explanation of how to housebreak a puppy (I guess she had or had

had an unhousebroken one). The powers that be then decided her interview was a bore (it was) and scrapped the whole thing. And the viewers get lucky and see another beer commercial.

Animals workers, humane workers, rescue workers, cat ladies, or whatever you wish to call them, remain misunderstood. Of course, a society in which they were understood probably would not need them. How do you like that "Catch 22" idea? Try it this way. Once upon a time the word *responsibility* meant "ability to respond." It was a very *positive* word used to describe an enlightened, functioning individual who saw things for what they were and had the ability to respond appropriately—period. In a society where the word had that meaning, obviously there would be many able to respond and share the work so that it would never reach overwhelming proportions.

But in a society like ours where responsibility is a negative word often indicating a burden we would rather avoid, there is no abundance of individuals "able to respond," so the work falls to the few, rather than the many, and there is of course more work because of society's general lack of responsibility. Those who are not part of the solution are part of the problem. So you have your "friendly neighborhood cat lady" who cares for the animals dumped by everyone else.

She has the guts not to walk away. She goes out during dangerous hours to dangerous places, trying to help animals the rest of society has turned callously away from. She spends almost all her income feeding, neutering, providing vet care. She is driven

to fill the gap between homeless animals and man. She does a good job. And if she's like most of the rescue workers I know, she also cares for a few elderly human shut-ins, waters everyone else's trees as well as her own, can always find a few dollars for a good cause, and supports herself and all the four-legged creatures she cares for, as well as her infirm mother or father or spouse or child.

No, she's not your ordinary neighbor. But since you may never get to know her as well as I do, let me acquaint you with her briefly through some sketches of my favorites (and unfavorites, too). (Names have been changed to protect their privacy.)

Helga and Robert

She—a breathless sweet lady in her late fifties—devotes her days to keeping a neat cat-filled house and feeding and trapping strays in the suburbs. He—a calm, tough, gentle man—works in the railroad yards, where he befriends and feeds strays, picking up and taking home those he can get close to. Often spends years getting to know a cat so as to pick it up. Adopting out those for whom homes can be found, keeping the rest. Obviously, cats are a great financial burden, and much is done without in order to care for the creatures. They have no car and travel in from the suburbs by bus with cats—she is a familiar sight with carrier and cane.

Maxwell

A very attractive gentleman musician in his mid-fifties, European-born, now friend to every needy

Cats are fed on pieces of cardboard, carefully picked up later so as to leave no litter.

soul in his neighborhood. Always tries to pick up calicos or tortoiseshell cats, knowing they are females and likely to be pregnant. Also, brings in cats belonging to generally careless owners and shopkeepers. One of our favorites because of his gentle, caring nature and kind personality. The type of person who insists upon paying in advance for every eventuality. It is so important to him to get the pregnant cats before they give birth that when on the one occasion a female turned out not to be pregnant, we scarcely had the heart to tell him.

Lillian

The cat-care lady, cycling around town feeding strays, caring for prominent people's cats in their homes while owners vacation or travel on business. Fifties, midwestern WASP ex-executive, able to talk anyone into or out of anything. Avid neuterer and declawer of cats who has learned the hard way about feline leukemia. Extraordinary ability and level of caring. Unfortunately, associates often drop away, overwhelmed by numbers of animals for which they find themselves responsible, most kept in an old apartment in a ghetto.

Sylvia

Mid-sixties, attractive, Australian-born eccentric maintaining personal cat shelter outside a metropolitan area from now-dead lover's estate. Often has one or two thousand cats and over one hundred dogs. Neutering, inoculating, and feline-leukemia testing generally lacking. Cats die in vast numbers daily in what is often called a "concentration camp for animals." Dogs ditto. Supposedly will adopt out, but actually will not release "my babies." Collects animals as some collect stamps. Houses them in somewhat converted chicken coops, reasonably clean, but diseases and pregnancy rampant. Encourages everyone to bring animals to her, including those that could easily stay in their current homes. People have no idea animals are actually going into a private prison. The scale of this venture is beyond comprehension if you have not seen it.

Victor

Mid-fifties accountant cum antique dealer renovating lovely brownstone he shares with a brother and two tenants in Brooklyn. Picks up homeless cats and dogs—forty cats and ten dogs in residence most of the time. All pets neutered; cats declawed; feline leukemia problem being treated with megavitamin therapy. Every pet named and responds to the name. House is clean; so are pets. Inoculations up to date, worming current, and so on. Willingly assumes a responsible caretaker role, which imposes great burdens. Adopts out only under very superior conditions. Very serious, feeling individual who probably says, "Why me, God?" at least ten times a day. Incapable of neglecting the needs of any living being even though the demands on him have reached an extraordinary level.

Evelyn

Fiftyish European-born masseuse devoted to a private cat refuge in New Jersey having over one hundred cats. Traps, feeds, and cares at a high level.

Roseann

City schoolteacher, braids, dungarees, and a cat carrier. Thirties, living in Brooklyn, married to an electrical engineer somewhat her senior. Picks up dogs and cats. Is the only cat person other than myself who has for years tested every cat for feline leukemia and now treats positives with megavitamin therapy. Often has ten to thirty cats in immaculate conditions. All dogs are housebroken and neutered, as are cats. Bears neutering, feline leukemia, and advertising expense herself. When she picks up dogs she cannot care for, calls the ASPCA for pickup. If cats are sick when brought to her or picked up by her, she euthanatizes them herself at home. Able to do this, but cannot cut a cat's nail so that it bleeds to get blood for a feline leukemia test!

Very clear in her own mind about her role as a rescue worker with both animals and children and understands it is the purpose of her life. Husband supportive and capable, also clear in his mind about the demands life has placed upon him as backup to her responsibilities.

Anthony and Esther

Mid-thirties Eastern European couple, residents in the United States many years, who consider animal work a spiritual journey and responsibility. Now have approximately forty cats and a few dogs. Most cats feline leukemia positive or exposed, carrying other diseases as well. All are neutered and being treated with natural foods, vitamins, roots, and herbs. Not using megavitamin supplement known to benefit feline leukemia and infectious peritonitis. Meditate with their cats, use pyramids, seek divine guidance. Now have household of illness into which no new cats should enter, none should leave because of contagion. "Natural" diet improving health of many.

Charlotte

A buoyant late-sixties saloonkeeper, quite a character in her wigs. Twice widowed. Was living in a modern West Side high rise with second husband and totally bedribben ninety-year-old mother. Picked up and housed many cats when living in a house in the East Thirties. Moved to the West Side with a few cats, continued picking up, did not neuter early enough, and overnight had almost thirty cats, what with three litters. Threatened with eviction, complaints to Board of Health and ASPCA, she contacted the clinic, which removed some twenty unneutered cats, neutered and returned the older cats, and kept for adoption fifteen young cats. More were adopted out from her home, so the numbers are now controllable and no more eviction threats likely. Was beginning to breathe easier and enjoy her cats. Stabbing death of her husband has now cut short peace of mind and stray work.

Pamela

Previously owner of a city grooming shop, she took in endless animals dumped by her neighbors. Formerly walked into the clinic with a dozen at a time. Gave up family and business to move to a very rustic animal refuge hundreds of miles away. A very harsh life in the wild for a fiftyish woman, caring for hundreds of pets abandoned by their owners.

Prudence

Attractive midwesterner of French descent, now in her seventies, with not a strand of gray in her long black hair. Has been befriending animals for over fifty years, keeps chickens, cats, dogs, squirrels, an occasional sheep, rabbits, birds in a house near the beach that could be mistaken for the neighborhood greenhouse. Feeds everything that walks on four legs or two. Lives with a very competitive animal activist who places severe limitations on her humane work. Prudence rarely neuters animals for adoption, hoping new owners will do so. Has not kept pace with needs for neutering, due to some degree to financial burdens imposed by common-law husband. Does not appear to understand strong feelings of other animal workers about lack of neutering on adoptions and permitting pregnant strays to bear litters that could have been avoided. At this point, Prudence is an anachronism, but a dear one.

Belinda

A still-beautiful lady in late sixties or possibly seventies who once worked in a hotel. Now says she tutors English. Certainly could; she speaks beautifully, although a bit breathlessly. Feeds cats on the streets of Hell's Kitchen, cooking food for them for hours at home before sallying out near midnight with an old shopping cart wired together to hold little containers of still-warm food and cool water. Her cats hear the squeaking of the cart and come running. Whenever she finds a home for one, she picks it up, stuffing it into an old lopsided carrier. Keeps many of her favorites at home, neutering only the males; females in season frequently, crying and urinating in her tiny old apartment. She means to get the females spayed but never quite has the money. Called one night to ask me where to call to have a body picked up. A battered, weak tom she picked up had died in her apartment. Told her to call Department of Sanitation. Later met her near her building, where she put body wrapped neatly in cat litter bag out on corner sidewalk as instructed by Sanitation. A sadness with it.

Lenore and Ellen

Sisters, nearly seventy, daughters of a famous musician, both musicians, gifted performers themselves, often performing for elderly or community groups throughout the city. Recently reunited after years of feuding; cats brought them back together. Take cats that others are "getting rid of" and have them spayed for adoption. Seem to get a lot of older cats. Having a hard time coming to grips with the need to care for each animal's total health problems, particularly those related to feline leukemia and infectious peritonitis. Evidently place many cats with their students. Have rarely seen them with male cats. Having some cats themselves but mostly turn over for adoption, paying all costs themselves.

Firemen and Cops

A common phone call to our clinic goes: "How late will someone be there to accept a cat for checkup and neutering? We just picked up this little gray kitty at the fire, and I want to get her in right away. But I can't leave the scene for a while. The fire's not out yet."

Policemen and firemen are a great group of rescue workers, keeping many of the animals they rescue and adopting out others, paying vet costs out of their own pockets. There may not be a Dalmation at the firehouse these days, but there's probably a cat at home!

Mariana

Judging by her son's age, must be in her early forties but never looks it. Superattractive blonde who started law school in her late thirties so as to handle cases for the elderly, the poor, women, and animal owners. Once had a private cat shelter housing some one hundred creatures in a city apartment, said to have been beautifully neat, clean, odor-free. She traps, neuters, declaws, feeds on the street. Bears tremendous expenses for cats of those unable or unwilling to pay. Not unusual to see her drop off a couple of cats for spay on the way home from a long day in court, looking just as neat as when she walked by at seven in the morning.

Maria

Fiftyish wife of a gentle, kind grocery-store keeper in East Harlem. Picks up roaming cats and dogs in droves; unfortunately, does not have the financial means or emotional strength to care for them as she would wish. But she's all there is for a stray animal in a very bad part of the world.

Nanette

Fifties, Swiss, immaculate, organized. Got started ten years ago feeding strays in downtown vacant lots. Arrived one morning to feed cats and found bulldozers at work bulldozing cats to pieces along with land. As pieces of cats flew, she realized she had to trap and remove strays on neighboring land before they too were bulldozed to pieces. Did so. To this day is particularly haunted by cats cemented in at construction projects and tries to get them out before cement is poured or will break through later if she hears a cat trapped inside concrete forms.

Feeds on the streets, in warehouses and apartment-house basements in most deserted parts as well as most populated areas of Manhattan. Traps everything she can, neuters, and returns wild cats to original locales. Places tame cats for adoption. Often brings in cats trapped in wee hours of the morning before going to office, where she holds an administrative position. Always perfectly, neatly dressed, no cat hair ever, although I know she has many cats at home, including wild ones. Bet no one at work knows where she is at 6 A.M. Income probably almost totally allotted to cleaning up the cat scene without killing. Will devote any amount of time and effort to trapping pregnant females. Always gets her cat.

Suzanna

State employee, married, now in her fifties living in netherlands of the city near the beach in house bought to allow keeping of large numbers of cats and a few dogs. Usually has thirty to forty cats. Bears most neutering, declaw, and advertising expenses herself to do adoptions as well as general veterinary care expenses of nonadoptables. Feeds on the street in her own neighborhood and traps whenever possible. Has lost large numbers of cats to feline leukemia. Fanatical about homes into which cats go; makes tremendous personal sacrifice to care for numbers of cats and treat feline-leukemia positives with megavitamin therapy. Always personally delivers cats for adoption so as to check out homes. Highly imaginative about names for cats.

My Aunt Mary

My late aunt—some fifty years my senior at the time of her death—married to a physician, residing in a beautiful old townhouse in Philadelphia when I was a child. The two of them, deliberately childless to leave them more time and energy to help others, aided poor German immigrants in the Kensington district and took in, fed, neutered, and cared for every dog or cat that came down the old carriage lane behind the house. Their own home was always immaculate, tastefully furnished, and full of the good odors of holiday dishes—never of animals! It was my favorite place as a child, but I had very little contact with the animals there since they were shut

out of the front part of the house when the family
came to visit. I suspect my aunt and uncle were
aware their relatives thought them "crazy" and simply sought to avoid confrontations. But my aunt did
write me very loving letters as the years went by,
detailing the regular trips to the vet to have each
animal cared for. I used to read with fascination
about Red's tail being amputated and Lilly's getting
her annual shots. When my father once commented
in a clearly disparaging tone that I was beginning to
sound like my Aunt Mary, I replied, "That's the
greatest compliment you can pay me." It's a comfort
to know that, well before she died, I had more than
taken up where she left off.

These are the "cat ladies." You'll notice they ask
nothing of you. But they do need the help of every
average pet owner.

They need you to neuter your own pet so that you
add nothing to their burden. They need you to take
in and care for the occasional friendly, lost cat who
comes to your door. They'll take care of the wild,
frightened ones and the ones in neighborhoods you
wouldn't dream of entering, the warehouse basements,
the abandoned tenements, the subway tunnels and
railroad yards.

Perhaps now you won't laugh the next time you
pass one of the cat ladies setting out little dishes of
cat food and water at a "feeding station." You may
even ask what you can do to help and not be deterred by the distance she puts between you and
her. If you cared to, you could buy some food or pay
to neuter a couple cats occasionally.

And with time the cat lady's face may become
familiar to you. I hope so. Because you may need

her when your begonia tree turns a little yellow and nothing the plant man tells you works. *She'll* know. And she may even let you adopt a kitten if you take good care of your plant.

INDEX

177